IN PRAISE OF HIDDENNESS

IN PRAISE OF HIDDENNESS

The Spirituality of the Camaldolese Hermits of Monte Corona

By A Camaldolese Hermit
Edited by Father Louis-Albert Lassus, O.P.

Ercam Editions
Bloomingdale, Ohio

Nihil Obstat and Imprimatur:
P. Lanfranco Longhi, E. C.
Superior Major

ISBN 978-0-9728132-4-2

Library of Congress Control Number: 2006924017

Front Cover: St. Romuald presenting the Order to Christ (Bieniszew)
Back Cover: Sacro Eremo Tuscolano

Printed in the United States of America

CONTENTS

Introduction 1

I   On the Paradox of Concealment 5

II The Solitary Cell: Our Divine Environment . . . 11

III The Prayer-Man: Concealment in God 21

IV The Man of Tears: Concealment in Misery 31

V   Daily Life: Concealment in the Commonplace . . .41

VI Solitude and Communion: Concealment in
    Ecclesial Communion 51

VII The Hermit, the Church, and the World 61

VIII What Joy! Christ is Risen! 71

Appendix —

    The Monastic Experience of St. Romuald (+1027):
    A New Interpretation of the Sources. 79

INTRODUCTION

By Friar Louis-Albert Lassus, O.P.

We have gathered here some spiritual conferences given to his brother hermits by their prior, who for many years has honored me with his faithful friendship. He has always been kind enough to send me copies with the idea that they might benefit me, which in any case gave me heartfelt joy. As the scribe noted in the Gospel (cf. Mt 13:52), my friend knows how to bring forth the spiritual treasures accumulated over a millennium (since 1027) by the sons of Romuald. He offers old things and new for the men and women of today fascinated by solitude, where God speaks to the heart and where the spirit of love brings one beyond all words into the enjoyment of the divine Reality. I asked his permission one day to publish the texts. It was not that easy to get it, and it was conceded under the condition that his name be omitted and kept between us. I agreed, realizing full well my limitations, my inability to express as he could that which he himself had lived for so many years.

In his conferences to the brother hermits, my friend liked to evoke some great themes of Camaldolese spirituality, as one tries to live it today in the few remaining hermitages of Blessed Paul Giustiniani (1476-1528) spread across the world. When on September 15, 1520, while he was Major of the holy hermitage of Camaldoli, Brother Paul left in the early morning like a thief, accompanied by a simple-hearted lay brother, it was not on a sudden impulse, but rather impelled by a heart overflowing with love and pain. For ten years this Venetian patrician was situated in this happy solitude, after having broken with so many persons he loved and with so many things to which he thought he had died. He embraced the initial stages in the desert with the folly of those "violent" for living the Kingdom of God. But now he knows that desert to be threatened, in danger, and he himself to be exposed, put on display, given over to the world of business and futilities. At Camaldoli he has published the Rule for hermits and recluses, brimming with the joy of the desert, for he wants to live and to make alive to the full the happy "disappearance" in Christ of the hermit, just as Romuald the contemplative and the first brethren of Camaldoli and of Fonteavellana lived it. Brother Paul wants to establish small hermitages, silent, hidden, concealed, poor, and joyous. For the eight remaining years that God is going to give him to live, he will organize this little eremitical family called today the Congregation of the Camaldolese Hermits of Monte Corona. Their ideal? To disappear with Christ in God, in the bosom of the Father, just as a drop of water disappears in an amphora of a precious wine, just as on August 7, 1524, Brother Paul disappears and is reduced to nothing at the hermitage of Pascelupo while celebrating Holy Mass. "I do not ask that your joy may penetrate me, but rather that I, like the faithful servant, may enter into it, and that reduced to nothing, annihilated to myself, I may taste Your love beyond all that can be said or understood."[1]

---

[1] *Secretum meum mihi* (Frascati, 1941), p. 53. This passage also appears on p. 384 of *Camaldolese Extraordinary* (Ercam Editions, Bloomingdale, 2003), hereafter cited as CE.

So we can say that the Camaldolese desert, like the Carthusian desert, is not only a matter of living *for* God, of living *with* God, of living *in* God, but above all of *living God*. This alone can explain that eminent form of this hidden existence that is reclusion, of which we have very recently a sublime example in the heart of Rome in the person of Sister Nazarena (1907-1990), or even again today in our brother Father John Mary at Monte Rua.

The conferences of my friend bear on some important aspects of this hiddenness in God: the meaning of the solitary cell, the increasingly interiorized prayer of the hermit, the hidden work of the poor, the tears of repentance and of tenderness ("the most beautiful ornament of the solitary") – and all this lived with the brother hermits, deep in the heart of the Church and of the world, pervaded by the very joy of God.

I

ON THE PARADOX
OF CONCEALMENT

In Communist countries not so long ago, the media never reported earthquakes, floods, train wrecks, disasters of all kinds, and other tragedies. Such occurrences were considered as the negation of the then prevailing dogma according to which the Soviet man must of necessity control all the events of the planet. The ideal of such a society being success, and a today always more glorious than yesterday, all disasters must therefore be concealed, denied. Catastrophes occur only in capitalist countries.

Now the society in which we live is in fact dominated by this same idol of success, of perpetual youth, of obligatory efficiency. Human pride, which tries strenuously to do without God and His laws, is unable to give meaning to earthly distresses and even simply to admit them. Among us, it is true that we are informed of our ordeals either by word of mouth, or by the press, radio, and television, but inevitably with indignation, protests, and accusations.

In short, the setback should not have occurred, and that is why we immediately look for the culprits that caused it. If something goes awry, then certainly somebody did not do his duty and should be condemned. For instance, it is even difficult to admit that an earthquake could not be foreseen and avoided. Why did not those responsible arrange everything so as to exclude all damage of goods and persons? Likewise regarding the recent bad floods. A number of mayors and magistrates expect proceedings to start against them. . . . It is certainly true that sometimes one sins by omission, but it seems that this clumsy search for culprits in all our misfortunes often has this strange idea as its underlying motive: man must be the absolute master of all, even of nature itself. To admit that certain calamities are natural and inevitable would be to agree that the human condition is fragile and, in the final reckoning, a state of death.

In the past, the faithful Christian accepted mishaps, seeing in trials a means God makes use of to punish us for our aberrations or to purify us and to prepare us for eternity. Today, a disaster is not seen at all as a challenge to faith or as a stimulus to abandon ourselves into God's hands, but rather just as a provocation to anger. Now anger supposes an enemy to shoot at, to unload on. Man's failure is a scandal and unacceptable. From the moment man wants to free himself from God, without really having the power, he needs to feel himself a victor. Success is for him more necessary than the air he breathes. He knows well, however, that "success" is not a name of God – at least not of the God of Christian revelation. But as in every error there is a grain of truth, so when the hour arrives that will put an end to history and reveal the Kingdom of God in all its grandeur, when at last the new heavens and the new earth will appear, it is then that we will be able to say that God's name is Victory. The idolatry of success in our wounded humanity reveals itself in the great illusion that tries to mask the enormous defeat called death. The human victories of science and technology vanish with this defeat, this last enemy that will be overcome by the resurrection of Christ.

The desire for success inscribed in the depths of our being is certainly not at all condemnable in itself, for it is the natural object of all we undertake, even if it is not always attained. Success in our existence represents, without a doubt, a true value, a good that we call "merit" in our Christian tradition. We have to "merit" heaven even though, in reality, it is a question of a gratuitous gift of God. But personal success is altogether compatible with material failure; the sick, the unfortunate, the handicapped can have a greater dignity, merit, and moral worth than the worth of celebrities written up in widely circulated newspapers. It is man's lot to live with failure, but likewise to lay hold of suffering and to use it as raw material for his human and divine success, his merit, his salvation, and his glory. Christianity, with the glorious Cross planted in its center, unlike Islam, is not a religion of "success". Yet the temptation certainly exists among us to want to establish God's Kingdom already on this earth. This is precisely, mark well, the temptation that Jesus repulsed in the desert at the beginning of His public ministry and preaching of the Gospel: "The Kingdom of God will not be realized through a historic triumph resulting from an ever-increasing ascendancy, but rather by God's victory over the ultimate unchaining of evil, which will make His Bride descend from heaven."[2] This is our hope.

---

[2]   *Catechism of the Catholic Church* (CCC), par. 677.

All these reflections on success and failure could appear far removed from our concrete life at the hermitage. But such is not the case. And it is not hard to draw from them some important, extremely useful lessons. The first is this: our departure for the hermitage is an eloquent rejection of the mentality of our environment. Our solitary life is not only a renunciation of the artificiality of a mundane existence based on appearance and efficiency, but it hides us from the eyes and the acquaintance of men in the heart of the mountain or the forest, in the heart of our cell, in such a way that we truly live concealed in complete anonymity. Jesus put this impulse in our heart, this yearning to disappear far from the competitive life of the world, so that we might grow day by day and at all costs in the truth of our being a man and a child of God. We said "yes", a "yes" that we repeat all along the way in spite of our frailty and the constant possibility of seduction by the artificial, or again, by the useful and the profitable. And so St. Peter Damian teaches:

> Even if today and tomorrow the hermit happily imprisons himself in his narrow desert cell, this is so that an immense dwelling may be prepared for him in heaven. Let him bind himself today to the solitude of the woods in the fear of the Lord so that he may taste true liberty. Resting in Christ, let him be a stranger to this world not only in body but in heart, according to the recommendation of the apostle John: "My little children, do not love the world, nor that which is in the world. If anyone loves the world, the love of the Father is not in him." (1 Jn 2:15) Thus he can cleave intimately and familiarly to his God.

Dead, he will live far from the dens of iniquity
of this world and, as if already in the grave, he
will repose in the sole desire of his Creator. And
his life, all hidden in God, will shine in splendor
when Christ will appear all radiant in glory.[3]

Meanwhile, note well that the totally hidden life that
God has chosen for us rises up paradoxically at the heart of
our world, troubled and torn apart, as a sign of freedom and
an emergency exit. Let us recall, moreover, the teaching of
our Blessed Brother Paul:

Most assuredly, one proclaims the Kingdom of
God loudly and effectively if he can affirm like
Christ: "My Kingdom is not of this world." He
cries out not only with his mouth, but with his
whole being: "I have no lasting city in this world;
I do not want to have in this life father, mother,
relatives, or friends. For I await another city in
heaven, not made by human hands, and therefore
I aspire and hope and run towards the Kingdom
of God."[4]

But here is another teaching. We all doubtless agree
with our Ancients who, fortified by their experiences, do
not hide from us the various difficulties that the hermit can
encounter in the course of his adventure of love. The cell
in the hermitage and the furnace of Babylon amount to the
same thing. The hermit knows better than anyone else his
weakness, frailty, timidity, cowardice, and that sluggishness
that seems to oppose itself to grace, and that lets us feel

---

[3] *Letter* 165.
[4] See also CE pp. 267-268.

how difficult it is to live the desert life day after day "with weapons in hand", as Thérèse of Lisieux says. All this risks discouraging us, if we are infected with the virus of success. Hence, so many brethren, after years of desert life, can call it quits, pick up their sheepskin, and return to the world – or, what in fact may be worse, can sink lamentably into carelessness, mediocrity, and misplaced sadness. O how urgent it is to take into account the daily lapses, tests, and apparent defeats in our life. All this lived in the light of the Cross of Jesus, in humility, patience, supplication ("Help me, help me," our recluse Sister Nazarena cried out constantly), can only transform itself into glory; but it takes time, persistence, and openness to the call of the hermitage and of Love.

I understand why our eremitical church at Monte Corona, like that of Camaldoli, is consecrated to the mystery of the Transfiguration. For it is necessary that a grain of wheat be hidden in the earth, and the hermit be hidden in his life, so that the sun of Jesus Christ may shine on the face of one who accepts death in order that he may live.

II

THE SOLITARY CELL: OUR DIVINE ENVIRONMENT

Go off into your remotest room
and carefully close the door. (Mt 6:6)

We know well that the architecture of our hermitages clearly differs from the cells of a Benedictine or Cistercian monastery, and likewise from a charterhouse. This difference lies principally in the absence of a cloister and the juxtaposition of the solitary cells with their little garden. These, together with the church, the chapter room, the refectory, and the common utilities, constitute our universe, the place where we live, and give it typically, in effect, the aspect of a little village or, if you prefer, of a Palestinian laura. This setup goes back to St. Romuald himself. As Bl. Rudolph relates for us in his shorter constitutions of Camaldoli,[5] written between 1080 and 1085: "Romuald, guided by the Holy Spirit, had five cells constructed where he placed five brothers, one of whom he named prior over the other four. He gave them the rule of fasting, silence and perseverance in the cell."

---

[5] Translation in *Camaldolese Spirituality*, edited by Peter-Damian Belisle (Ercam Editions, 2007).

So what distinguishes a Romualdian hermitage is the cell, with its four small rooms and its central corridor. The oratory, where the hermit can celebrate his solitary Mass is certainly the holy of holies of the little house, hiding place of the solitary. Camaldoli, just like Fonteavellana, is meant to be a colony of hermits, a "bivouac" of God's soldiers, according to St. Peter Damian's beautiful expression.[6] Yes, it is truly the solitary cell that, in the Romualdian tradition, comes to define, form, and express the brother-hermit who occupies it. That is why, in the eyes of our cardinal-hermit, attentive and loving disciple of Romuald, hermits are those "who live in a cell," those who "love the cell," those who "are happy in the cell."[7] Likewise, each brother inhabits a cell separated from the others, from which he comes out only for communal acts, for the community's material and spiritual needs, or for his own.[8]

The upshot of these texts, and of many others, is that "remaining seated in the cell" constitutes definitively the formal element of our life, the indispensable and fortunate condition of our "disappearance", of our "concealment". "Nothing", our Blessed Brother Paul states, "is more normal and necessary for those who practice *hesychia* [stillness] than to remain in the cell, seated and in silence."[9] Therefore, the "custody of the cell", that is, to spend the greater part of the day in the cell, gives us the "right" to call ourselves hermits even if we live with our brethren. "Just as the occupation of the priest is to celebrate the sacrifice of the Mass, and of the doctor to teach, so the ministry of the hermit is to remain

---

[6] *Letter* 28:46. See also Belisle, op.cit.
[7] *Letter* 50:9.
[8] Coronese Constitutions 11.
[9] See also CE p. 457.

seated in silence and in fasting," declares St. Peter Damian.[10]
"Therefore, the hermit should not leave his cell," he adds, "if
he wishes to bear the Lord's yoke in peace. This continual
retirement fills the soul with light."[11] We knew (at least
some among us) Dom Odo, who was Major during the
difficult years of the Second World War. "The spirit of our
eremitical family," he used to say, "is a virginal flower. If it
is not jealously guarded, if the hermit does not stand aloof
from dangerous or simply futile excuses in order to keep his
solitude, the flower wilts, dries up, and dies."[12]

Besides, the institution of an eremitism designed for
a multiplicity of persons has always been an undertaking
requiring a delicate balance. This explains why, in the
course of the centuries, such foundations were few in
number and did not really survive, except for the venerable
Order of the Carthusians and our own. Hence, our ancient
fathers have well said that to transform a hermitage into
a monastery is like passing from the monastery to the
life of the world. If we want to protect and develop our
Romualdian charism (and such is our duty before God,
the Church, and the world), then we have to commit
ourselves with earnestness and generosity to rediscovering
if necessary, or to enhancing, the meaning and value of
our solitary cell. This is not the unique dimension of our
life, but it is the most specific and the most often exposed
to rough handling. Recall the exploit of the unfortunate
Teuzone, who established his eremitic cell at the very heart
of Florence. Catastrophe is inevitable and the hermit, this

---

[10] *Letter* 50:13.
[11] *Letter* 165.
[12] *Camaldolese Questions* (Frascati) p.8.

brave man clothed as a monk, has nothing left but the name and the beard. . . .

It was precisely to make possible and to maintain the permanence of the hermit in his cell that, until recent years, the institution of lay brothers existed. Less bound to their cell than their brother clerics, they took charge of the biggest part of the material tasks of the hermitage thanks to their manual labor that was often heavy, but carried out with love through their vocation in service to the contemplative life of the hermits properly speaking. For various reasons, in the spirit of the postconciliar reform, today our eremitical family no longer knows these two types of Camaldolese life. It was certainly a risky enterprise. The General Chapter that made the decision gambled big with the contemplative tone of the hermitage, and it certainly did not take long to perceive this. Henceforth, the duty of remaining in the solitary cell holds for all the brother hermits, whether clerics or not, as does at the same time the obligation to participate integrally in the celebration of the Liturgy of the Hours and to contribute to all the offices of the hermitage and to all the works that serve the common good. The courageous and perilous decision to unite clerics and lay brothers can and ought to be considered as a quite fortunate event from many points of view. However, in all sincerity, we cannot avoid stating that it has given rise to real difficulties in preserving and authentically living the characteristic qualities of our solitary life, and in particular, fidelity to the cell, with its silent peace and its continual prayer.

And so for instance, the hermits today are much less in their solitary cell than formerly, seeing as most of the time the work is accomplished outside the cell. But what is extremely dangerous is thus to habituate oneself easily to living on the outside. We are dealing here with a temptation well known to the ancients and to our first Fathers. We have to adapt a wholly new psychology regarding this terrible and sacred place where Jesus awaits us to speak to our heart and where, little by little, day after day, man lets himself be worked on by the Holy Spirit so as to become a desert, capable of receiving all the fullness of God. Even if the cell is not an absolute, the hermit must be occupied by the desire to return to it as quickly as possible whenever obedience leads him outside it. That is why our Fathers say flatly that "the cell left for a brief moment is regained with greater joy, but abandoned often and for a rather long time it is little by little neglected and even risks becoming an insupportable torment." I think of our dear cardinal-hermit Peter Damian, so often torn away from solitude by Hildebrand, his "holy Satan", for the service of the Church. What saved his contemplative life was his deep devotion to his cell at Fonteavellana, about which he made this magnificent confession:

> Just like a sick man who entering an inn is healed of his languors and infirmities even before taking anything, so did it happen with me. As soon as I reached the threshold of my cell, without needing to open some book or other, but marvelously by the very virtue of the place, I found myself safe and sound, healed of all my wounds. I recovered my health while recovering the holy books, though still closed, as though finding myself before a vessel containing my remedy, which enveloped me with the perfume of its aromatic plants.[13]

---

[13] *Letter* 6:5.

Furthermore, you know that each time he entered his cell, Peter Damian embraced the door as if it were his spouse.

One must certainly not absolutize the solitary cell. The Blessed Brother Paul himself considered as fully adapted to our way of life places like the hermitage of St. Jerome at Pascelupo or the Grottoes of Massaccio, which do not allow separate cells on account of the cramped terrain. And in describing the recently built holy hermitage of Monte Corona, Luke of Spain, author of the first history of the Camaldolese Hermits, written in 1587, notes that vocations were so numerous that it was necessary to put together two or three brothers in each cell while awaiting the construction of new hermitages. And the chronicles tell us plainly how those men became true contemplatives and saints. This leads us to reflect that the spirituality of the cell can be lived in different ways, while reaffirming that the solitary cell in our traditional Camaldolese laura favors to the utmost full union with God. Hence, it evidently deserves our preference and our noblest desire.

But I would now like to recall a comment that I have sometimes heard on the lips of a brother and that often reminds me of the attitude of some of us who are more attracted to passing their "free time" before the Eucharistic tabernacle of the hermitage's church than to staying hidden in the secret of the cell. It is certainly quite possible that certain ones among us regret not being able to devote themselves for a long time to adoration in the Presence of the Lord in the church. The sensibility of the soul of each of us is very personal and ought to be respected as much as possible. However, the theologians can help us to see the matter clearly, and this is what they say: The precise aim for which Jesus wished to make Himself present in the Eucharist was not so much the adoration of believers as fusion with each and all in Holy Communion. Ultimately, Jesus comes to make of each of us the privileged place of encounter with the most Holy Trinity. "If anyone loves me," He says, "my Father will love him, and we will come to him and make our abode with him." (Jn 14:23) Now it is precisely recollection in the cell that can bring us, little by little, into harmony with this mysterious and blessed presence in us of the Trinity.

There can be no question here at all of an anti-Eucharistic reaction, but of a serious awareness of our tremendous wealth as baptized, unceasingly renewed and fortified by communion in the Body and Blood of Christ. Now permanence in that divine place that is precisely the cell, in silence, despoilment, and austerity, cannot but favor a closer, more stable, and more constant union with God. Our observances are certainly broad enough to allow us to go to prostrate ourselves before the tabernacle or to remain hidden in the cell, even though the latter manner of acting corresponds more naturally to the line of our eremitical vocation. And that is the reason why, for example, we are not allowed to make our *lectio divina* habitually in church. In the long run, the cell would risk being considered a profane place for eating and sleeping rather than the "parlor of the Holy Spirit", as St. Damian so rightly calls it.

When I am alone in cell, I realize that at every moment I am borne, pardoned, called by God alone. And at the same time I belong to the brethren, the Church, and the suffering world, just as they belong to me in the light of faith and the strength of love. Surely an education is necessary. Little by little, the cell reveals itself and commits to us its mystery, provided we hold out in it. At first it seems to be shut up within the horizons of the world, but in reality it situates us more and more in God and thus at the center of human history.

Even if the Ancients repeat that the cell teaches everything, this holds true only under the condition that the hermit perseveres therein. With their common sense, they believe that, humanly speaking, the solitary life cannot satisfy anybody. This is why William of St. Thierry can tell us wisely: "Solitude and reclusion are words of misery." For this reason, those who intend to give themselves definitively to our vocation should have a sufficiently long experience of the hardships of such an existence. Even though our Rule permits us real moments of relaxation, and the liturgical year offers a rich variety of feasts and seasons, these cannot eliminate the fundamental poverty, the sobriety, and the despoilment of our daily life. It is during the latter that the rightness of the eulogy of the solitary life left us by St. Peter Damian becomes manifest. For a long time one might have thought that it was only "literature". Afterwards, one fine day, the veil is rent and one is overwhelmed by the sweetness of the place, by the sweetness of God.

In conclusion, let us listen to the moving testimony of St. Peter Damian:

> O hermitage, only those who know you, who rest sweetly in your arms, can tell of your grandeur and chant your praises. As for me, I only know this and affirm it in all sincerity: 'Whoever forces himself with perseverance to enter more and more into the desire to love you will finally enter

your mystery and, at the same time, the mystery of God'.[14]

We belong to the race of the brethren of Camaldoli, of Monte Corona, of all our venerable hermitages, which were great places of silent, hidden love.

---

[14] *Letter* 28:52-53.

III

The Prayer-Man:
Concealment in God

When we speak about our life to the rare visitors to our hermitages, it happens rather frequently that somebody asks us the question: "And how many hours of prayer do you have each day?" I am in habit of responding: "24 out of 24". At least it ought to be so. And I add that for every Christian the commandment of the Lord holds: "Pray without ceasing."

Yes, indeed, the hermit's "specialty", his "work", is this pure and continual prayer of which St. John Cassian speaks, and which he tells us is the end of all monastic life. It is contemplation, it is the invasion of the Kingdom, or rather, according to the thought of our Brother Paul, entry into the Kingdom. We know well that it is much more than life with God or life for God: rather it is to live in-God, to live-God. Let us recall the remark of Thomas of Celano about St. Francis: "He was not so much a man of prayer as a prayer-man. He became prayer."[15] Such is the dream of the hermit, the result of a whole life of faithfulness in the grip of the Holy Spirit, the "doorkeeper of the Kingdom".

---

[15] *Second Life*, n. 95.

With her usual outspokenness, our recluse sister Nazarena forcefully reminds us:

> In a contemplative order like ours, the contemplatives ought to be the rule and not the exception. The hermits must at all costs be men of God, without which the Camaldolese cage will be peopled not with bold eagles, meant to fly high up in the sky, but by harmless and timid doves, without daring, circling back and falling down exhausted.[16]

Nazarena has firmly grasped that the end of a hermitage is neither penance, nor work, nor the cloister, but rather that life in-God, that God-life, which is in accordance with the logic of our baptism and with the tremendous desire of our God to communicate Himself to us in order to divinize us, in the strongest sense of the term.

Three biblical texts can help us considerably to pinpoint this contemplation of God and to assign it its beautiful Christian quality. First of all, a word from Deuteronomy which, for that matter, recurs constantly in biblical teaching: "Remember. . . ." (Dt 8:2,18, and passim); then, there is the recommendation of Jesus: "Watch and pray at all times" (Lk 21:36); and finally, the sublime invitation of the discourse at the Last Supper: "Abide in me, abide in my love" (Jn 15:4, 9).

"Remember. . . ." The masters of the spiritual life insist strongly, following Deuteronomy and the prophets, on the urgent necessity of retaining the remembrance of God and of the marvels of His mercy in our regard. We are all forgetful,

---

16 L. A. Lassus, *Nazarena*, p. 108.

distracted, scatterbrained, in the multiplicity of the things and the activities of the world. And so we are little attentive to Him who alone *is*, in whom we have being, life, and movement (Acts 17:28), who envelops us with His presence of immensity, to be sure, but even more in the depths of our soul with His presence of love. "At the origin of humanity," says St. Gregory of Sinai, "forgetfulness obliterated the remembrance of God. And man violated his orders and discovered his nakedness."[17] "Remember all the way that the Lord, your God, made you journey for forty years in the desert: to test you, to humble you, to make you feel hunger . . . but also to give you manna which neither you nor your fathers had known. . . . And tell me, my people, did your feet swell during those forty years? Did your sandals wear out?" (Dt 8:2-5)

For we too forget all this history of mercy toward humanity. "The duty of remembering!" This is precisely why we have dragged ourselves away from diversions, from the enormous cavalcade of the carnival of men. We are hidden in the desert in order to become *hesychasts*, interior men, men of inward unity and peace. We aim to live, after St. Benedict's example, "under the gaze of God, so as to set our heart on heaven."[18]

It is precisely to keep constantly this remembrance of God that we occupy ourselves daily with *lectio divina*. We live it inside that tent of meeting of which the book of Exodus speaks, where God used to converse with His servant Moses face to face, mouth to mouth, "as a man with his friend" (Ex

---

[17] *On Commandments and Doctrines*, 17.
[18] St. Gregory the Great, *Dialogues* 2:3.

33:11). The Camaldolese hermit is a man of the Bible, as was St. Romuald, and as our Blessed Brother Paul requires us to become. St. Peter Damian says in turn: "Therefore, always have these pages [of the Bible] in your hands. Let your heart be constantly occupied with reading the divine volumes. Dwell in them, make them your abode, persevere with tenacity, a tenacity of unceasing vigilance."[19] Or again:

> Let us go further forward unceasingly into the fields of the Word, walking therein with happiness. You may run there with full freedom across the spaces of the sacred texts. Thanks to the intuitions of the mystical intelligence, it will even be possible for us to reach in some way as far as the summits of the steep rocks. There we will enjoy the sweet conversation of the saints, the serene joy of the eternal banquet.[20]

Who among us, after some years of faithfully rummaging through the "coffers of the Holy Spirit", will not taste something of this sort of divine enchantment? "Ah, what a beautiful God we have! – *O Bonitas!*"

And now here is the second text, put forward by the Lord Himself: "Watch and pray at all times." (Lk 21:36) I ask myself if we take seriously enough our condition as wayfarers, as pilgrims, as nomads of God, and thus as watchmen in this ephemeral world, which has the right to ask us: "Watchman, what of the night?" (Is 21:11) Such a state of affairs calls out to us constantly to be more and more, in our entire behavior, free men like the nomads are. But at the same time, it changes

---

[19]   *Letter* 6:29.
[20]   *Letter* 165.

our mentality to that of men waiting and watching, who sleep but very little even as our ancient fathers did, getting up in the middle of the night to hasten the return and implore the Hour – "Come, Lord Jesus!" (Apoc 22:20) – while being ready to receive Him when He comes. The ancient monks, just like our first brother Christians, asked with cries from the heart for the coming of the Kingdom of their dear Lord, and this waiting was the same as an ecclesial ministry. They safeguarded the Church's inspiration, always more or less tempted by complacency. Their life was, then, a continual prayer, faced with the possibility of the imminent return of Jesus in His glory.

This continual prayer of the hermit is comparable to the panting of certain thirsty animals who long, sometimes even violently, to reach at last the spring of living water. "What a sublime spectacle," sings St. Peter Damian,

> when the recluse hermit in his cell chants the nocturnal psalmody, like a sentinel in front of the camp of God keeping vigil attentively over the soldiers' sleep! While he contemplates the course of the stars in heaven, his lips unfold the procession of the psalms, which advance towards their term at the break of dawn.[21]

And finally, our third text: "Abide, then, in my love." (Jn 15:9) We feel keenly that we are here at the very heart of the continual prayer of the hermit. It is the translation, the interiorized expression – ever more simple – of a love that is communion, fusion, participation in the Trinitarian festival. The word "abide" is known to be a term characteristic of the

---

[21] *Letter* 28:58.

Johannine theology. It indicates quite precisely the condition of a baby on its mother's breast. So it does not signify merely a presence of God, but a close and permanent vital dependence. And it is precisely this intimate and permanent fusion of God and the soul of the hermit that is the ontological foundation of continual prayer, "I in Thee, Thou in me" till one arrives at the "Thou" alone of St. Francis of Assisi or of our Brother Paul. Perhaps we recall the radio message of Pius XII of July 26, 1958: "Such is the heart of the contemplative life, to abide in God in love so that God abides in us." And he added, "Our daily life has no other aim than to bring our mind and our heart into an ever more intimate union with the Lord."

The model of such a prayer without words, which is nothing other than to live-God, is without any doubt Jesus Himself. "Philip, have I been with you so long a time and yet you do not know me? Do you not know that I am in the Father and the Father is in me?" (Jn 14:9-10) Now through grace, His friends and brothers, such as ourselves, participate in this intimacy. "You are always with me and all that is mine is yours." (Lk 15:31) And thus the hermit enters into this continual prayer of Christ, into this continual ebb and flow of love in the Holy Spirit. "The Holy Spirit prays in us," says St. Paul, "coming to our aid in our weakness." (Rom 8:26) So we hermits, or in any case we who wish to become true hermits, are among God's privileged ones.

If it is true that the place for prayer for each one is the environment in which he lives, then the hermitage is par excellence that chosen land where we can not so much live for God, or live with God, as live-God. The solitude and the separation from the world, together with the silence that envelops our lives, are among the most favorable conditions for living in deep recollection. Added to this is the very presence of our brother-hermits, to that degree that all and each are animated by the same desire for union with God, seeking His face in all truth and simplicity. Cassian sagely tells us: "The supreme goal to which the monk tends, the summit of the perfection of his heart, is indeed the union of his heart with his Lord".[22] Perhaps it is not superfluous to repeat that our work, which at times is intense, is not at all in itself an obstacle to this continual and pure prayer of vigilance and love.

Yet even more than these material activities, which often even help us to meet God and to be with Him, there are "thoughts" that assail us and hinder our prayer. And that is why our Father Romuald recommends: "Leave behind you the whole world and the memory of it; be attentive to your thoughts like a skilled fisherman is attentive to the fish."[23] The image Romuald uses is known to be quite traditional. And so we can read in the *Ladder* of St. John Climacus: "The vigilant monk is a fisher of thoughts, skilled in spotting them in the calm of the night and catching them."[24] "It is a question," Evagrius says on his part, "of discerning the thoughts which arise in our head, ordered of themselves to prayer but mingled with some bad thoughts." It depends to a great extent on ourselves to determine the quality of our thoughts and to decide whether or not they should be given hospitality within our heart. It is, as a matter of fact, in the

---

[22] *Conference* I, 7.

[23] St. Bruno of Querfurt, *Life of the Five Brothers* (V5F) 2, 35. Cf. CE p. 489, and Belisle, op.cit.

[24] Step 20. See also CE p. 502.

interior of our heart that the quality of our thought and prayer is revealed. He prays continually who keeps his heart and imagination clean of thoughts of anger, faultfinding, suspicion, bitterness, contempt of a brother, etc. Nobody can live in union with God if, for example, his fraternal relations are continually conflictual or marked by a cold disinterest. For leading well our contemplative life, fraternal charity, humility, and obedience are no doubt just as important as our silent solitude.

Thomas Merton tells us:

> Very few men are sanctified in isolation, very few are
> perfected in absolute solitude. To live with others,
> to learn to forget ourselves out of understanding
> for their weakness and faults, this can help us to
> become true contemplatives. For there is no better
> means to rid ourselves of rigidity, hardness, and
> the crassness of our entrenched egoism, which is a
> huge obstacle to the light and the infused action of
> the Holy Spirit. Even the courageous acceptance
> of interior trials in an absolute solitude cannot
> totally compensate for the work of purification
> accomplished in us by humility and patience in
> loving other men, our brothers.

Likewise, there should be no need to recall that one does not achieve prayer straight off. It takes time, constancy, and patience. The wisdom of the Church's tradition tells us rightly that prayer is impossible if one does not strive to pray at certain established moments, which are peak times by reason of the intensity and the duration of prayer. And I think it is in that perspective that we must grasp one of the meanings of the *Opus Dei* that punctuates each day spent in the hermitage. In itself our liturgical Office, celebrated calmly and soberly as our Ancients wanted, is continual prayer. However, it would be wrong to consider it sufficient for acquiring the *habitus* of being in God. God is all, and the only homage adequate to Him is that of all our time. By withdrawing into solitude, the hermit can actualize prayer more easily, even if he does not celebrate the canonical Hours. These, in any case, "must be considered as the piles of a bridge thrown over the course of time. These supports have no other purpose than to hold up the road, which spans the river and connects the two banks."[25]

If such is truly one of the advantageous aspects of our liturgical stopping places before God, then we better comprehend an ancient observance of Camaldoli that Blessed Paul Giustiniani reports to us:

> Let us consider this as extremely important: in going to church for the celebration of the Hours, whether going from the cell to the church or returning from the church to the cell, keep an absolute silence. Especially when leaving the church, regardless of the Hour that one came to celebrate, let each return to his cell in great silence. May it never enter anybody's head to go anywhere else than to cell, or to address a word to a brother.[26]

This could seem to be a rule that unnecessarily complicates life. In reality, it protects the purpose of our eremitical life, I mean continual prayer and being in God.

---

[25] Adalbert de Vogüé.
[26] See also CE p. 459.

The canonical Hours are the halts of love and praise of God. It would be quite illogical, then, to make use of them to ask for some news or to have a discussion with the brethren, even about things pertinent to the progress of the hermitage. If, before or after the Divine Office, one easily gives in to the desire to talk, the effect of the Office will be practically nil. I doubt it would be possible for us to practice this observance punctiliously today, but why not try it?

Finally, I would like to note that, although continual prayer serves as the ideal of each and every one of us, to achieve it is above all a grace, a marvelous gift that God has in store abundantly for some among us. These are the hermit brothers whom we call "prayer-men": I mean brothers who not only pray much and willingly, even perhaps in dryness and without particular enjoyment, but, even more, brethren deeply marked by their assiduous contact with God and radiant with faith, humility, interiority, serenity, and that inner festivity that shone on the face of our father St. Romuald. I thank the Lord for having been able to discover in our various hermitages some of these men who have passed over entirely into prayer. May it please God that we all might become such. That could only be the fruit of humble persistence in love and of the transforming action of the Holy Spirit, who teaches us to cry out: *Abba, Abba* (Father, Father).

IV

THE MAN OF TEARS:
CONCEALMENT IN MISERY

One is really lucky to have as master and friend a man who has wept much. Scarcely anybody but children and saints weep without shame, and St. Romuald was both at the same time. The floodgates were opened one fine day when the man of God happened to be at Parenzo and read Psalm 31: "I made known to You my sin, O Everlasting! And I said, 'I will confess my transgressions to the Everlasting,' and He wiped away the penalty of my sin." (Ps 31[32]:5)[27] There was a veritable deluge of tears, of repentance, and of tenderness. The tears would never stop flowing, especially while celebrating Mass, or when at times, "like a seraphim of love", he spoke of Jesus. Since then, tears have become one of the marks of the Camaldolese hermit, as we are told by St. Peter Damian,[28] or again by the chronicles of the first disciples of Brother Paul Giustiniani. It is urgent for us to remember, and indeed to beg from God, this inestimable gift, that is part of the grace of the desert. It would seem that our path of conversion, as it brings us ever nearer to God, distances us to the same degree from our sin and the sin of

---

[27] Cf. St. Peter Damian, *Life of St. Romuald* (VR), 31. See also Belisle, op. cit.
[28] *Letter* 153.

the world. So it would seem logical that there could no longer be any question of aught but fullness and joy.

Now in reality, things are not so simple. Certainly, the hermit who progressively draws near to the Lord his whole life long is less liable to fail in love through sin, but at the same time, and in a paradoxical fashion, he learns more and more what sin means, his own and that of the world. Yes, closeness to God and the rejection of sin increase or decrease together. Those we call "sinners", among whom we evidently are included, do not truly realize what sin means, while the saints, as for instance our Peter Damian, declare themselves basically "sinners", beggars of mercy. The discovery of God, who is absolute holiness and above all love, throws light on our basic impurity and on our refusal to love. In this light we cannot but declare ourselves unworthy of Him, just like the prophet Isaiah at the time of his vision in the Temple: "Woe is me! I am a man of unclean lips." (Is 6:5) And we cry out like Peter at the time of the miraculous catch of fish: "Depart from me, Lord, I am nothing but a sinner." (Lk 5:8) It is so true that to see oneself in the light of God is to "measure one's emptiness and imperfection".[29] Such an experience cannot but strengthen our relationship with God: "Our attraction to God and confidence in Him will be so much the greater the more deeply we feel and experience our misery and our impotence!"[30] Let us call to mind the prayer of our Brother Paul:

> Lord, I dare not say to You: "Show me the light,
> that I may believe in Your light"; but it is enough
> for me that You make me see my darkness. . . .

---

[29] Constit. 33.
[30] Ibid.

Bring me back to myself. In my misery, I have distanced myself not only from You but from myself, becoming a stranger to myself. Make me know my darkness, that then I may look at the light. Yes, I tell You and repeat to You incessantly: "Show me to myself, so that I may know my sins."[31]

It can happen that we fashion for ourselves false ideas of the contemplative life to which we are called at the hermitage, so that we may expect more or less happy and pleasant experiences. In reality (let us not delude ourselves), we are going to experience (oh how much) that we have been called to the desert in the first place so that we might be humbled, so that we might learn to be hungry. "That is what you are!" Remember certain apothegms of the Fathers who practiced sobriety, for example: "The devil, transformed into an angel of light, appeared to one of the brethren and said to him: 'I am Gabriel, and I have been sent to you.' The brother replied: 'Make sure that you have not been sent to some other brother. As for me, I am absolutely unworthy of such a thing.' At once the devil disappeared." Or again: "Someone asked an elder how certain ones could say: 'We have visions of angels.' He retorted: 'Blessed rather is he who sees his sins without ceasing.'"

And let us not think that having such a keen sense of our sins might be an obstacle on our path of contemplation. Just the opposite, as our Blessed Brother Paul so well reminds us:

Nothing is more efficacious in helping us penetrate God's world than awareness of our own wretchedness and that kind of disquiet which we

---

[31] See also CE pp. 368-369.

feel because of our sins. The spirit of a man who feels himself weighed down and crushed by so many miseries is necessarily pushed toward prayer. From self-knowledge springs true humility, without which it is impossible to please God. I would not be able to express by word or writing the various kinds of prayer which consciousness of our misery may engender, but I am convinced that there is no better prayer than that of the hermit who becomes able to pour out from his eyes a flood of tears of compunction and who burns with desire for the heavenly fatherland.[32]

One could certainly raise some objections, today more than ever before, to cultivating such a state of the soul. For example, the following: Authenticity, sincerity, and truth are beyond doubt essential requirements for our relationship with God. Now if I do not have a sense of sin, do I have to demand of myself just the same this spiritual attitude completely foreign to me? What then of my sincerity? Must I artificially cultivate anguish and fear before a God-truth, in order to afterwards free myself from these sentiments at the heralding of a God-father of mercies, always ready to forgive? What is the good of this hot and cold shower?

Or again, this query: Am I an inferior monk solely because I don't seem to correspond to the classical definition of him "who weeps for himself and his brethren"?

These are surely serious questions that call for serious answers to those posing them. Men generally differ from one another, and monks likewise. Hence, it may happen that at the hermitage there are those who have not yet shaken

---

[32] *Trattato sull'orazione*, Monte Rua, 1983, pp. 41-42.

themselves free of a rather sad past, while others seem up to a point as if they had been preserved from all sin. The majority, however, are situated at a midpoint between these two extremes. Now it is pretty clear that often we do not give in to temptation precisely because none arises, but we realize then that we can be sinners without committing sin. "If we say we are without sin, we deceive ourselves and the truth is not in us. If we acknowledge our sins, He who is faithful and just will forgive us." (1 Jn 1:8-9)

So the brother who has not gotten to the point of seeing this deep-down misery in himself, the wounds inherent in our human condition, should endeavor to come to this blessed discovery evidently still more through prayer than through introspection. "If you are not yet able to shed tears for your sins," St. John Climacus tells us, "weep at least because you are unable." Yes, this revelation is the fruit of a true grace of God that our fathers never hesitated to ask for with insistence, while begging at the same time for the gift of tears:

> Did they not cleanse the public woman of all her stains? Did they not allow impure hands to touch not only the feet but also the head of the Lord? Did they not grant it to the renegade apostle not only not to perish after his lapse but to obtain the primacy over all the senators of the celestial court? Yes, they purify the soul from the stain of sin and steady the wavering heart in prayer. They transform sadness into joy and, while running from our fleshy eyes, they turn us to the hope of heaven.[33]

---

[33] St. Peter Damian, *Letter* 153.

If it is true that we are witnessing today an appalling loss of the sense of sin, due to many factors, it would be truly sad if monks and hermits let themselves be contaminated by so unhealthy a virus. Even if the sin exists, the possibilities for no longer considering it as such are enormous today, facilitated by a certain mentality that more or less readily judges any lapse normal and denies all personal responsibility. I do not think that it would raise anybody's dignity to reduce adults to the babyhood of those who "do not yet know how to distinguish their right hand from their left." It is true that sin should disappear – but not through dissembling and explaining it away, but rather through repentance, conversion of heart, and God's forgiveness.

There certainly can be false expressions of the sense of sin. In fact, sin is not just the transgression of established norms and precepts, but much more the breaking off of a relationship of personal love. Each of us is a sinner before God. Regarding an impersonal law, there can only be transgressions. Now in many one discovers a morbid sense of guilt that ought not to be confused with compunction of heart. A true sense of sin urges one to confident prayer, while a morbid sense of guilt rejects it. A true sense of sin opens up the way to repentance, because at the same time that one commits the fault – if not even before committing it – one is aware of the love of God, who pardons and transforms.

The feeling of being a sinner, accompanied by a continual need of God's loving forgiveness, contributes enormously to our progress on the way of God's commandments. In fact, there is a progression in the way we correspond to the demands of holiness, not in the sense that certain commandments are less binding than others, but that progressives such as ourselves advance by stages. Normally, taking a once-and-for-all decision is not sufficient for reaching sanctity. It is necessary to go forward without ceasing in order not to stop and, above all, not to fall back. Now to know oneself imperfect, weak, a sinner, and to accept all this while trying to do better what until now was done badly – this is Christian realism and this is humility, that "door of heaven" as the Ancients call it.

We must truly accept being like the publican, even though we may be tempted to ape the Pharisee: "O God, I thank You that I am not like others." Like him, we may wish to keep all the rules, but a condition like his is so abominable in God's eyes! How preferable it is to humbly recognize one's miseries, like the publican, and to throw oneself upon the mercy of God. Staretz Silouan of Athos tells us this profound word: "The son asks forgiveness for his sin, the slave looks for excuses." It is precisely forgiveness asked for and obtained that gives us a tangible feeling that we are esteemed and loved, whereas the pretense of doing quite well as hermits takes this joy from us and shuts us up in isolation.

To be sure, it is painful to admit that one is a sinner. Nevertheless, the sense of our sin is not necessarily a sad and discouraging experience. Quite to the contrary, it will often be a source of peace and joy. Is not a sin acknowledged and repented of already a sin forgiven? And if there is joy in heaven over one repentant sinner, why should not this joy abide in the heart of him who repents? This is why St. John Climacus also speaks about *penthos* [mourning] that is transformed into joy, and why the tears of compunction of our father St. Romuald at Parenzo were changed into tears of tenderness and happiness.

But now I would like to point out a marvelous consequence the sense of our sin has in the area of our relations with our brethren and of the compassion for the world that we are responsible for bearing. Compunction of heart cannot but make peace grow in our neighborly relations, for it makes us lose the desire to criticize and condemn our brethren. Whoever knows that he is deep down a sinner "in the first person" feels it out of place to occupy himself with the faults of others. . . . If it is his duty, he does it because it is his ministry, and always with mercy, humility, understanding, and compassion. We lose our peace too often by attaching too great an importance to the lapses of the brethren or of those in charge at the hermitage. We want a better world, and we are right, but we must think first about improving ourselves. Only one who knows by experience his own limitations can effectively contemplate improving his life's milieu. Otherwise, he will risk stirring up bother and confusion.

One remembers the words of John Paul II: "Recovering a correct sense of sin is of first importance in confronting the grave spiritual crisis that man is experiencing in our time." Surely, it is clear that the profundity of our life in Christ cannot be reduced to this. There are so many other aspects, and how important they are, but in any case compunction of heart remains always the solid foundation of our entire life of union with God. This compunction shows us what an enormous difference there is between Christian contemplation and non-Christian Eastern spirituality. We cannot imagine a Hindu guru or a Zen monk expressing himself on his spiritual experiences as, for instance, St. Isaac of Nineveh does: "One who knows his sin is greater than one who raises the dead through prayer. One who knows his own weakness is greater than one who contemplates the angels."[34]

This is precisely what explains the self-effacement, the gentleness, the overwhelming goodness of hermits like our father Romuald or, much nearer to us in time, Saints Seraphim of Sarov or Silouan. They saw their troubled faces transfigured, while yet on earth, into faces of glory.

---

[34] *Discourse* I, 65.

V

Daily Life:
Concealment in the Commonplace

Somebody has said: "The poetry of the monastic life is its prose." Yes, this is quite true, but it takes quite some time to understand and admit it. Before entering the hermitage or charterhouse, we generally think that from now on we will be occupied with sublime activities and that at last we will live with exceptional men. Now our day is all made up of little things, often quite humdrum, which are going to be repeated tomorrow, and the day after tomorrow . . . until death, or thereabouts. As for our fathers and brothers, we soon enough discover them to be limited like us, imperfect, wounded, and sinners like us. What a surprise! But no, we would be realistic, and we accept with good humor such an unexpected situation. It is the path of life and holiness.

Let us take, for example, our work: so humble, even sometimes so banal! Some years ago, a tastefully edited brochure from one of our hermitages, which aimed at presenting our kind of life, made no mention of the daily work that the hermits carry out. Nevertheless, our Constitutions say clearly: "Work makes up an integral part of our days."[35] And they even devote several articles to it.

---

[35] Art. 51.

The fact that our solitary life "wholly oriented toward union with God in contemplative prayer"[36] foresees that all hermits be occupied several hours each day in manual or intellectual work for the service of the community[37] is not at all seen as subtracting from our contemplative life. There certainly were, and still are, forms of solitary life that refuse work as being a "possible obstacle" to union with God, and that repeat Jesus' saying: "Do not work for the food that passes away." (Jn 6:27) But in our Camaldolese hermitages, animated by the spirit of St. Romuald, it is not like this. With us, work has always had an important place. Let us remember the little eremitical colony in the vicinity of St. Michael of Cuxa. St. Peter Damian reminds us that, "for three years, Romuald and John Gradenigo worked the earth with a plow, sowing wheat, and thus lived by the work of their hands."[38] So also later, at the hermitage of Pereo, "crafts were substituted for agricultural work. All the brethren devoted themselves to manual work, some making wooden cutlery, others spinning, still others making fishing nets."[39] At Camaldoli in the eleventh century, the Constitutions ascribed to Bl. Rudolph determined that "the hermits will sometimes work outside their cell, for instance for the harvesting of vegetables and fruit, haymaking, or again to cultivate the garden."[40]

So as we see, in the primitive hermitages they engaged in work activities that certainly did not constitute a significant contribution to the economic life of the time, as was to be the

---

[36] Art. 9.
[37] Cf. Art. 12.
[38] VR 6.
[39] Ibid., 26.
[40] *Constitutions* of Bl. Rudolph, ch. 34-35.

case with the Cistercians in the twelfth century. Far from it! But our works are carried out quite simply to submit our body to the law of work, such as we discover it in the first pages of Genesis, where we see man placed upon the earth to "cultivate" it and to keep it (Gn 2:15). Since, then, work constitutes a fundamental given of human existence, it is quite normal that we should love it as an element of our education and our achievement. Moreover, the Second Vatican Council recalls that "religious should obey the common law of work and thus provide for themselves the necessary means for their subsistence, while banishing all exaggerated preoccupation from their heart and committing themselves to the solicitude of our heavenly Father."[41] To live from one's work, as the poor who earn their bread – this is a noble resolution for a monastic community. Certainly experience shows us that, today more than ever, our work cannot fully support us – far from it – and we need the help of our friends and benefactors. But happy are we if we can, each according to his ability and strength, face up to life without resorting to subterfuges.

On the other hand, this is what our Brother Paul Giustiniani observes: "Work, even when not indispensable to the economic life of the hermitage, is not only useful but necessary to avoid idleness [*otiositas*], the enemy of our soul."[42] Now we sometimes think that to go places in our prayer life, it is urgent, or at least desirable, to have plenty of time to ourselves for reading and for study, time untrammeled by manual occupations. But our precursors in the solitary life were not at all of this opinion. In fact, they considered *otium*

---

[41] *Perfectae Caritatis*, 13.
[42] See also CE p. 462.

a danger for the soul, and work not so much as an obstacle to the life of prayer, but rather as a means of staying united to God without distraction. St. Jerome wrote this to the monk Rusticus: "Always keep at some manual work, so that the devil always finds you busy."[43] This is equally the opinion of Cassian, who passes on to us a maxim of the Fathers of Egypt: "The monk who is working is tormented only by a single demon, but the idle monk by a legion."[44] We could interpret this saying in the following manner: One who works has fewer obstacles to get clear of, so as to keep united to God, than one who is idle. Blessed Brother Paul also recommends: "Each brother ought to so conduct himself that there is always more work left for him to do than he has time to finish."[45] We remark at the same time that, according to his opinion, these activities include not only material tasks, but also the components of the contemplative life: *lectio*, study, psalmody, prayer.

This, moreover, is what Blessed Paul tells us on the subject of study:

> The hermits are allowed to devote themselves to
> any study which the Church does not forbid, but
> it is clear that those who study Holy Scripture
> rather than profane letters will have chosen the
> better part . . . without forgetting [if studying a
> secular subject] that their object should remain
> the attainment of a deep familiarity with the
> Word of God.[46]

---

[43] *Letter* 125:11. See also CE p. 466.
[44] *Instit.* 10:23.
[45] Constit. 30. See also CE p. 466.
[46] See also CE pp. 450-451.

Likewise, he states: "Experience has shown that, for religious souls, study stimulates all the virtues."[47]

If now we ask the monastic tradition what relationship there is between prayer and work, we get, broadly, three answers: either alternation, or compenetration, or opposition. By contrast, we never come across the strange idea, which has arisen only recently, that work is in itself prayer, and that, consequently, explicit prayer is superfluous.

The alternation of work/prayer found its happiest formulation in the Rule of St. Benedict. Certainly, St. Antony had already learned from an angel so to alternate times of prayer with times of work in order to remedy the temptation to acedia. In his eyes, fatigue in prayer springs from the continual attention of the mind. Now this fatigue is surely lightened by work that plays a relaxing role, without, however, becoming a diversion. "Our material occupations," our Constitutions say, "are ordered to our spiritual activities. Hence it is legitimate that, being in cell, we sometimes prefer a very simple manual task to give rest to the spirit. Sometimes this work is an anchor that fixes our spirit, for it checks the fluctuation of thoughts and permits the heart to remain united to God for a longer time without weariness."[48] Experience clearly shows that this is the case. Is not the daily timetable itself the expression of this alternation: "Prayer/work"? On the other hand, the continual union of the soul with God in the image of the communion of Jesus with His Father should certainly be the ideal of each one of us, and thus the liturgical hours that articulate our day aim at

---

[47]   Ibid., p. 452.
[48]   Art. 35.

contributing to giving our work and all our other occupations their quality of service of God, in peace and silence.

In the eyes of the Ancients, there is neither separation nor opposition between *hesychia* and work. At times, it is true, we lament having too much work (which certainly can happen) and think that it hinders our living as true contemplatives, but perhaps the solution lies precisely in the contemplative fashion in which we perform it. One day, Thomas Merton made this remark: "In our monasteries, certain religious do everything with the mindset of a worker, prayer included, while others do everything as men of prayer." And what we do is less important than the way in which we carry it out. Of certain brothers, I could affirm what John Cassian wrote of certain monks in Egypt:

> It is not easy to say to what their interior joy should be attributed, whether to their application without respite to their manual labor, thanks to their fervor of spirit, or to their acquisition of extraordinary graces of light and of experience of God, thanks to their perseverance.[49]

What, then, will our spirituality of work be? Our Blessed Brother Paul thinks that nothing hinders us from being united with God in work, even if all too often we have the contrary experience. It is not at all work itself that hinders union with the Lord, but that which often accompanies it: frivolous and pointless chatter, grumbling, criticism, rash judgments, daydreams, and interior cinema. Therefore he recommends to us the chanting of the "divine canticles", meditation on the Word of God that chases "thoughts" from

---

[49] *Instit.* 2, 14.

our heart and very gently keeps us present to what is essential. "A peaceful occupation", say the Fathers, is rest in God. Look out for frenzy in work, for the sort of voracity that at certain times betrays emptiness of heart, boredom in the silence of the cell, the temptation to flee to the world. But there can also be, at times, a sort of vainglory in comparison with the brethren: "I am the one who keeps this place going, who feeds the community." Nothing could be more deadly for our interior life of freedom than a brother pleased with his usefulness.

After these theoretical reflections, I would now like to say something about the concrete works that we maintain in our hermitages. Obviously, we exclude all those that are truly incompatible with our solitary vocation. For instance, our Constitutions say: "Our hermit priests are not allowed to exercise a ministry outside the hermitage, even if the needs of the active apostolate might call for it."[50] Or again: "No work is acceptable at the hermitage which could disturb the solitude, our place to search for God."[51] This text is certainly quite clear, but its application can sometimes prove difficult. Thus, for example, although nobody likes the noise of a tractor or chain saw, their discreet use seems to be admissible to a certain extent. It is also stressed that "the hermits should seek out the humblest and most despised tasks."[52] What is meant here seems to be those activities that perhaps offer no particular satisfaction, but that are absolutely indispensable for the well being of the brethren of the hermitage. I mean, for instance, the preparation of meals; doing laundry; sweeping; keeping

---

[50] Art. 87.
[51] Art. 126.
[52] See also CE p. 464.

the cell, the garden, and the whole house tidy; and other such occupations. These, indeed, are tasks from which the hermits ought never to be excused. These are occupations that are, in fact, not only useful, but also necessary, and altogether compatible with communion with God.

Such communion is certainly possible, even if it is true that only part of our work is performed in secret in the solitary cell (which is the ideal). And yet the cell is never forgotten. We all have the duty to keep our cell neat, and to clean, cultivate, and adorn the little garden attached to the cell. We also have to do some personal laundry, repair this or that, etc. It would be truly sad if the activities done outside the cell would not allow us this type of work. That would sound the alarm of a dangerous imbalance in our solitary life, and all the more so because to give oneself to some peaceful work in cell entails a very special grace.

And we must not forget, finally, that care for the beauty of the hermitage of which our Constitutions speak and which must be the object of the concern of all the brethren. This is an aspect of our work that cannot but make us think of the Japanese Zen monasteries, where the monks, pruning shears in hand, tend the marvelous gardens that surround the monastery. Our hermitages must be places of beauty: first of all, surely, of spiritual beauty that shines in the faces of the hermits, without forgetting aesthetic and material beauty. Tidiness, order, and good taste exert more of an influence than we realize on our souls and the souls of those persons who come to us.

Because our communities nearly always have only a few hermits, our work is almost never for profit. It is limited to making possible the peaceful progression of our life. And for this, blessed be the Lord! At the end of our course, perhaps we will have the impression of having "empty hands", or in any case, of the banality of our days. But what of it? At Nazareth, in the hiddenness of the everyday, holiness was not sought *from* things, but *in the midst of* things. Love alone gives life value.

VI

SOLITUDE AND COMMUNION:
CONCEALMENT IN ECCLESIAL
COMMUNION

We are living at a moment in history in which the sense of belonging [*les appartenances*] is eroding. Individuals are losing their roots, I mean their bonds with that social ground that not only transmits life, but permits a healthy and strong development. We are witnessing an enormous breach with tradition on the national, social, family, and religious level. This is doubtless a phenomenon comparable to the epoch of the migration of peoples at the end of the ancient world, even if the reasons for it are completely different. Today, it is not a question of the barbarian invasion of a society that is fading away, but of the quickening development of "modernity", of the invasion of the mass media, and of the death and resurrection of ideologies.

This context, which strangely throws out of kilter our accustomed state of affairs, cannot leave us indifferent, for it is in this selfsame world of ours that we are going to have to live out our life in Christ in the desert. It is clear that our belonging to Christ saves us from being totally uprooted. By grace, we stand forth as "Sons of God", and not as the product of chance and nothingness. We "know" our Father.

Admittedly some, trying to make a virtue of necessity, greet the absence of social, moral, religious bonds as a veritable liberation. The simple act of fitting into previous traditions seems to them a restriction to their personal freedom. But does not their way of thinking and their behavior conjure up the parable of the prodigal son? We might ask ourselves which of the two brothers enjoyed a more authentic freedom. Was it the one who always stayed home, or rather the junior who, after a brief time of freedom, found himself in the darkest misery and aspired to become the last of the hired hands who worked at his father's house, that father to whom he could have been an heir? It seems to me that belonging, if it be freely accepted, definitely builds up true freedom. "My child," says the father to his elder son, "you are always with me, and all that is mine is yours." (Lk15:21)

Our fundamental belonging is surely our relation to God. It comes entirely from His salvific initiative. It is He Who in Jesus has freed us from the powers of darkness and has transferred us into His Kingdom (cf. Col 1:13). "He loved us first," (1 Jn 4:1) and hence it is up to us to adhere to this divine call with gratitude and faith. Baptism and monastic profession have consecrated this belonging to Jesus Christ. This present condition requires being lived out in an existence of unconditional obedience. *Ego vobis, vos mihi* ("I to Thee, Thou to me." Cf. Cant 2:16). Jesus Himself is our incomparable model. "I always do what is pleasing to my Father" (Jn 8:29) – so much so that, between Him and His Father, there is perfect agreement: "All that is Thine is mine." (Jn 17:10)

The monk just as well, following the logic of his name

(which includes a whole program of unity and unification), seeks therefore to immerse himself in the exclusive belonging of Jesus to His Father. He does not want to belong to himself, nor to other masters, but to God alone and with an undivided heart. "The unmarried man," says St. Paul, "is concerned with the Lord's affairs. He seeks how to please the Lord." (1 Cor 7:32)

Now, do we really occupy ourselves with thus pleasing the Lord? It seems that the dominant spiritual climate, even for Christians – I dare not say monks – manifests other orientations. First, we display an extreme individualism. It is not so much God who is of interest to us, to speak with Him and to belong to Him, but rather we look for a personal experience, we shut ourselves up in our own spiritual search that we call "transcendental meditation", or "depth meditation", or something completely different. Let us admit that, at present, a spiritual self-centeredness reigns, which arises from the current opinion that the world is only an appearance and that, basically, the self and God coincide.

If the supreme criterion of life in Christ is no longer adherence in faith to the Triune God, but personal experience, the change to a religious syncretism will be quickly made. And we know that the supposition of syncretism is precisely relativism to the subject of all that concerns the fundamental question of man. Alas, we frequently encounter today brother Christians wedded to the mentality of those people who are quite skeptical when faced with divine Revelation presenting itself as the absolute truth. Many consider all religions as equivalent, all as "true", but conceived only as a collection of signs and symbols, and all unjust and arrogant as soon as they do not content themselves with this role assigned to them.

It would be serious if we Christian hermits let ourselves be contaminated by such a mentality, so widespread today. It is true that our Church rejects nothing of what is true and sound in the non-Christian religions. So there is nothing to marvel at if, for example, one of us reads with profit the Hindu texts. "Examine all things," says St. Paul, "keep all that is good." (1 Th 5:21) This could hold as a valid standard for our reading. It is allowed and even necessary to dialogue with non-Christians. But in this encounter, it is not possible for us to be silent about what we have seen and heard concerning the Word of life, who revealed Himself before our eyes (cf. 1 Jn 1:1).

On the other hand, we cannot belong to God and please Him without the mediation of Jesus Christ. "There is only one God and only one mediator between God and men, the God-man Christ, who delivered Himself up for the redemption of all." (1Tim 2:5) We are saved, redeemed by the sacrifice of Jesus, which is precisely the principle and the cause of our belonging to Him. "Do you not see that you are no longer your own, in your body? . . . So glorify the Lord with joy and gratitude." (1 Cor 6:19)

It is wonderful to belong to Jesus. Although, without any doubt, we take a rightful pride in our "freedom", which is a free gift from God, this pride is far exceeded by the exhilarating experience of having made a gift of that freedom to Him who loves us. And again, let us note well that this belonging to Christ is both exclusive and inclusive. It certainly excludes any other master than Jesus, but includes all men, who are loved by Christ and who could, in fact, be excluded from our heart. It includes, in particular and obviously, His mystical Body, the Church. We are by no means solitary individualists, dedicating ourselves for some reason or other to a purely personal spiritual search. In spite of our material solitude, we are part of the people that God acquired so that they might proclaim His marvels: "He who called us out of darkness into His wonderful light." (1 Pt 2:9) We can say that, in the bosom of the Church, contemplative communities live their belonging to Christ and to His Church in a particularly explicit way, by proclaiming more by their existence than with words the wonders of the history of God in His dealings with men.

Nonetheless, the gift of ourselves, expressed by our monastic profession, inaugurates a new belonging, one which, to be precise, binds us to the community where the will of God has put us. Our Order, our Congregation, our Hermitage is this religious Reality to which He has mysteriously called us – these brethren who like us are invited to live together in our different hermitages, where this Reality is incarnated, is articulated, and moves in the holy "everyday". This belonging is the precise object of our vow of stability in the family of the Camaldolese hermits. And it is thus that we belong to God, to Christ, and to the Church. This is the result of our free gift, the source of a constant increase of joy and of freedom.

It is certainly quite possible to belong to God, to Christ, and to the Church without belonging to our family or to any other. But once this belonging has been realized and accepted by each one and by the whole body of the hermits, it becomes the concrete expression, now constituent and no longer optional, of our belonging to God, to Christ, and to His Church. "What God has joined together, let no man put asunder." (Mt 19:6) Those words spoken by the Lord concerning marriage are just as valid for us if we apply them to our membership in the family of the Camaldolese hermits. The conjugal consent of the spouses is not solely a contract between two persons. If it were, it could be broken off with the agreement of the interested parties. But Jesus affirms that this contract is the work of God and Himself and hence cannot be revoked by men. Knowing, then, that a divorce could never constitute a practicable solution, the spouses have at their disposal a strength and a powerful help to be able to get past their eventual differences. And it is the same way with membership to our eremitic Congregation. Even if, apparently, there is just a reciprocal relationship between persons, nevertheless it includes a dimension of the divine order. If, in fact, we are convinced that God has called us here – and the perpetual profession gives an almost certain guarantee of this – then we can be sure that God will assist us in getting past temptations and in fulfilling our contract of love.

Membership in the family of St. Romuald expresses itself, among other things, in fidelity to certain exterior signs: the habit, the tonsure, the beard, but above all in the love of our traditions, of our Rule, and of our observances. It is not an easy thing for anybody. Some brethren ask themselves whether fitting themselves into a tradition established for centuries, into a well-structured community, does not mean the extinguishing of the individual's personality. This is, surely, a realistic and doubtless necessary question. Whoever wishes to become a member of our congregation must consider well during the course of his years of formation whether his eventual profession will stifle his personality or bring it to full bloom. Discernment on this point is not always easy, for to encounter some difficulties does not necessarily imply that one must choose another path that will put an end to them. It may even signify the contrary, an invitation to surpass them, which could allow for surmounting these difficulties positively and even eliminating them.

Even after perpetual profession, it is quite possible that the temptation will present itself that one made a big mistake and hence must change his direction. In nearly all such cases, it is a question of a malignant suggestion that we must reject. The eremitical profession, received by the People of God, is certainly a sufficient indication to enable one to continue tranquilly on the road taken. Moreover, to be able to alter at this point in time the commitment made, one needs unequivocal signs. Now who would dare deny that there are cases of escape, of culpable flight?

If it is necessary in the interest of all to defend the bonds we have contracted, this does not mean that a formal and existential belonging would be sufficient. It is quite possible to be just wearing an eremitic "mask", even for long periods of time. "They went out from among us," says St. John, "but they did not belong to us; otherwise, they would have remained with us. It only served to show that they did not belong to us." (1 Jn 2:19) This "extraneousness" may be completely masked by a correct attitude, very reasonable and even pious, without the whole person being deeply affected by it. "There is a way of looking, of judging from the outside: of evaluating, calculating, and organizing oneself," the

Cistercian abbess Piccardo[53] observes. Now if that is possible when somebody is living in a Trappistine monastery, with how much more reason can it happen among us, seeing as our semi-eremitical life gives us a wide berth wherein each of us can move about and systematize things freely for himself.

That is just why our fathers since Romuald and St. Peter Damian insist so strongly on the importance of obedience in our solitary life. It really makes no sense for a brother to live physically in the hermitage, even adapting himself more or less to the common observance, while leading his private life without any desire to give himself and to truly open himself with simplicity and generosity to his brethren. He claims himself so much "in love with silence and the cell" that he always keeps the latter firmly locked, and woe to the prior who would dare to visit him, as our constitutions precisely require. Woe if he is asked to change cell or hermitage. Woe to him who has the gall to ask him to do a task during the time of repose, etc. There are religious who seem to be constantly bustling and on the defensive against the aggressions of the prior and the brethren. Truly they have understood nothing of what it means "no longer to belong to oneself", but to God and to those who are the sacrament of His presence. If such behavior became the general rule of the hermitage, it would cease to be a family of hermits and would be transformed into a more or less pious bachelors' club.

Doubtless, the community in which we live constitutes a very precious and effective help for our growth in union with God, the aim of our life. It is the surroundings we need "to hate our own life in this world, and to keep it for eternal

---

[53] *Alla scuola della libertà* (1992), p. 37.

life." (Jn 12:25) Now this community is not respected at all if we take advantage of it, if we make it serve our "I" so as to egotistically realize our "personality" by means of it. On the other hand, we can be sure of finding God and of realizing ourselves in the community if we give ourselves to it without thinking too much of what it will give us in return.

The contemplation of the Word of God, who at Christmas became a tiny babe who did not speak, fills us with amazement and gratitude. His abasement pushes us to "have the same feelings" (Phil 2:5) that were His, and without a doubt we will also have the experience that there is "more joy in giving than in receiving." (Acts 20:35) If the gift of a glass of cold water will have its recompense from God, nobody here must be afraid to lose by giving himself over to Him and to his brethren forever. He will get back beyond all expectation.

VII

The Hermit, the Church, and the World

I do not think it superfluous to ask ourselves seriously what the Church and the world might mean for us, and what we, hermits and sons of St. Romuald, might represent in the eyes of the Church and the world of today. Surely, this is not a new question, but it is one that demands ever more timely answers, answers more in accord with our concrete situation and that of our world.

The Second Vatican Council tells us plainly: "Since the contemplative life belongs to the fullness of the presence of the Church in the world, it needs to be implanted everywhere."[54] We can and ought to ask ourselves the reason why.

It is possible to discover monks of the past who, in their writings, hardly showed themselves to be particularly interested in the interrelationship of the monastic life, the Church, and the world. Certainly, we cannot ascribe this shortcoming to a lack of a sense of responsibility, but likely rather to the fact that one does not speak, or speaks very little, of what is self-evident and of first importance. It only becomes urgent to speak of the oxygen in the air when

---

[54] *Ad Gentes* 18.

it is lacking. It is given us in abundance, so we do not even mention it.

However that may be, our holy Camaldolese fathers themselves had an amazingly keen sense of this Body of Christ that we form, as their lives and their writings clearly show. St. Peter Damian and our blessed Brother Paul Giustiniani, among others, made each in his own time important contributions toward theologically situating the solitary life in the Church. Their arguments can be quite striking in their timeliness, and it is certainly good for us to draw profit from them.

As his name already indicates, the monk – man of solitude – basically seeks to become a close friend of God. He tends to realize in an imminent fashion the spiritual, personal dimension of the individual that each one of us is. Now in today's world, this choice of a personal vocation is, alas, often not understood. It was necessary that the "Pope of human rights" raise his voice to defend this right of the human person, doubtless the most fundamental. Addressing contemplatives at Lisieux in 1981, John Paul II told them:

> Do not try in the slightest to justify yourselves. All love, from the fact that it is authentic, can and must find justification in itself. . . . To love gratuitously is an inalienable right of the human person, and, it must be added, above all when the being loved is God Himself. . . . Under the guidance of the contemplatives and mystics of all times, continue to bear witness forcefully and humbly to the transcendental dimension of the human person, created in the likeness of God and called to live intimately with Him.

In these words of the Holy Father, it is easy for us to catch a glimpse of the Lord Jesus, who did not fail to defend Mary of Bethany, the contemplative, against the protests of her sister and, later, of Judas Iscariot: "Everywhere throughout the world, where the Gospel will be preached, they will tell what she has done for me." (Mk 14:4)

Our vocation to the solitary life evidently presupposes our belonging to the Church and to the world. Before being hermits we are Christians, and we have much more in common with a Christian like us who is not a hermit, than with a hermit who is not a Christian. That is why monks have always tried to view their life in the light of the Church and of humanity. St. John Cassian, for example, endeavors to show that the monastic life is in direct continuity with the primitive community of Jerusalem. Even if this thesis, historically speaking, is untenable, still it constitutes a precious witness of the sense of the Church in a monastic author who is a direct heir of the desert fathers.

For St. Peter Damian, the being of the Church is constituted by a concord in faith and love, in such a way that our material separation from other Christians by no means hinders our real unity with all the brethren. This is, as we know, the theme of the famous Opuscule XI, *Dominus Vobiscum*,[55] the very place where Peter Damian intones the most beautiful hymn in all monastic literature in praise of the solitary life.

However, reflection on the dimension of the Church in our life is not solely useful for justifying our contemplative life, hidden in silence, in the eyes of our contemporaries, but

---

[55] *Letter* 28.

in our own eyes as well. Tempted by some demon or other, we can sometimes start to doubt the choice that we made, and that was confirmed by the People of God.

And so we start to consider as a mere "stage" a commitment that, by its very nature, is meant to endure until death. The truth is that what troubles us at these moments is our small number, and certain features of our life that make us so different from our contemporaries, so "strange". A community that devotes itself mainly to prayer and contemplation – what does *that* mean? Is it not totally outside the categories of modernity?

To face up to such a tempest of thoughts, we need to realize more than ever that what should serve to explain us is not precisely "doing", or "producing", but "being". Sons of St. Romuald, we have heard the call to disappear, just like bandits who hide out, and like lovers. Hermits themselves are in fact lovers who have opted for the shade, for the life hidden with Jesus in God . . . the *vita umbratilis* of the Ancients. So we need to accept and love the meaninglessness of our choice in the eyes of those who judge according to the wisdom of this world: It should suffice us to be known by God.

This means, in the concrete, that we should free ourselves from the details of history and not trouble ourselves about them in the least. For as the Jewish scholar Abraham J. Heschel explains in his fine book on the Sabbath, "there are two types of history: One where the silent presence of God is made vain by the presumption of man; the other which is 'His' history through man." It is up to man, that is to each one of us, to play his part by embracing every day his vocation on earth. This is extremely important and explains the insistence of the pastors of the Church that monasteries and hermitages ought to flourish all over the world. For example, Paul VI says: "Monks, far from being absent from the life of the Church, on the contrary are situated right in her heart." And what is this heart of the Church, if not the new life in Christ and the intimate and constant union of this new man with his dear Lord? To say it once again, such is the end of our life at the hermitage. It is not among the "useful" realities, but rather I dare say, among the "super-useful", just like the deed of Mary of Bethany, wasting on Christ's feet the costly perfume.

We have not been begotten by our holy father Romuald to take up a specific "service" in the Church, as a Dominican assumes the office of preaching. But this does not mean at all that our solitary life is not, in a certain sense, a ministry, as is every other form of life that wants to be faithful to the Gospel. Prayer is our sacrifice, the contemplation of God our silent witness – yes, all this – and we must thus live intensely for the world of men, our brothers. And then Life will overflow into the Church and humanity. Do we really believe this? Let us recall rather what Moses told Pharaoh: "Let my people go into the desert to celebrate there a feast in my honor." (Ex 5:1) This meant nothing to Pharaoh, for in his eyes to serve God meant merely to indulge in unjustifiable laziness. And hence his response: "Return, then, rather to your work. It is because you are lazy that you say: 'Let us go to offer a sacrifice to the Lord in the desert.' " I really think that today, as in the past, serving God is considered by most people (and sometimes by ourselves) as an activity devoid of significance, since the only things that count are production and consumption.

Under such conditions how can we expect thanksgiving – the pure praise sung to God "because of His boundless glory" – to spring up and grow, and what meaning can a life totally dedicated to this have? And how can we agree that the doxology ascends to God with still greater disinterest and strength when it rises up from the bosom of abjection and suffering? However, we should not forget that the canticle of creation (Dn 3:23f, Gk.) was struck up by the three young men, thrown into the furnace and dancing, with a mysterious fourth man who had joined them . . . that the *Spiritual Canticle* of St. John of the Cross came to birth in the infamous dungeon of Toledo . . . and finally that the *Canticle of Brother Sun* of the Poverello of Assisi sprang from the faith of Francis in Crucified Love. Till the end of time, our world is in the pangs of birth, and the presence of hermits and monks should make it shine with the theological virtue of hope, which awaits God from God.

But let us go still further. In our hermitages, as we know, there are sometimes some truly magnificent brothers, real masterpieces of the Holy Spirit. Besides them, there are other brothers who have not yet totally surrendered their being and their activity to the action of grace. But we are together, and it is possible for us to speak about a communitarian sanctity, which can be a powerful and liberating sign in our world. We bear witness together to the Kingdom of God, because it is our absolute and unique future. Usually, it is true, a witness has seen what others do not know. Now it is up to us to announce precisely what "the eye of man has not seen, what his ear has not heard, what his heart cannot even suspect." How is this possible, if not because "God hath revealed it to us through the Spirit"? (1 Cor 2:9-10) Whoever renounces certain great and true earthly values for the sake of this Kingdom becomes, in truth, its witness, and all of us together, the great and the not so great, renew our holocaust "for the sake of God's Kingdom". Our Brother Paul writes:

> We quite readily forsake all the pleasures of this life, because we have the Kingdom of Heaven ever present to the enlightened eyes of our heart ... I say that in our era there is no truer, more effective way to announce the Kingdom to the world than to become a hermit.[56]

Our world scarcely wants to bother facing the fact that it is created. It even pretends to be a creator and wants to attain its perfection with no reference to transcendence. Likewise, our contemporaries sharply resent the affirmation made by our bare and joyful life of its precariousness and its ephemeral character, its relativity and its limits, seeing this as a sort of scandalous aggression. But does it not also pose a question? This is what enables us to affirm that it is urgent for the People of God to announce by word, and still more by example, that man, that humanity and the cosmos, can only fully realize themselves in and through transcendence.

Monasticism, and in particular eremitism, wants to declare loudly that man, every man, is so much more than a product, so much more than an object to be consumed and then thrown away when no longer of any use. Anyway, we are witnessing a healthy reaction to this mentality, but unfortunately one led astray through a swarm of sects and so-called Gnostic movements. For men do not easily let themselves be reduced to their material dimensions. Religiosity is always alive and well, but very often it lives

---

[56] See also CE p. 269.

outside the Churches. We cannot be unaware that there is a whole spiritual supermarket, well stocked with a variety of products: religions old and new, different psychosomatic techniques, and meditations of all kinds. It seems to me that all these phenomena present a challenge to the Christian contemplative monastic life, and a pressing invitation to live to the full what our fathers St. Romuald, St. Peter Damian, Brother Paul, and the saintly Camaldolese rank and file have bequeathed us. We are being asked to give testimony to the interior life in the midst of a world that has forgotten it, or rather that seeks it, but in the wrong way.

It is true that quite quickly we feel our impotence. We would so want to help, to intervene, and we do not know how. And sometimes we feel ourselves blameworthy because we are sheltered from so much of the suffering that marks so harshly the existence of so many of our brothers and sisters. We can and we must very strongly affirm our love and our compassion in their regard. But what should we do for them, and how should we do it? It is then that intercessory prayer and supplication well up of themselves. Of course, we will not be able to ascertain their efficacy, but we must leave it all up to the almighty mercy of our God. Paul VI said to our Camaldolese sisters on the Aventine: "One does not go to prayer as placidly as when one chats with friends. You should bear in your hearts the whole passion of the world."[57] "We who are strong have the duty to bear the infirmity of the weak," (Rom 15:1) said St. Paul. Just as Christ, the preeminently Strong, bore in His Passion the weight of us all, likewise those who follow Jesus very closely become, in

---

[57]   February 22, 1966.

a certain way and to a certain measure, similar to Him by making their own the burdens of others. Yes, it is precisely to a participation in the Cross of Christ that monks and hermits are called, for the sake of the Church and for the sake of the world. This is an intercession that is expressed less by words than by one's life. Divo Barsotti says: "Prayer is not only speaking to God on behalf of men, it is also 'paying' for men." In agreement with him is our dear Silouan: "To pray for men is to give of one's heart's blood."

Let us recall what our Constitutions have to say about the sick and the old of our eremitical family: "Suffering makes us like the sorrowing Christ and associates us with the work of the Redemption by uniting us intimately to the whole Mystical Body."[58] The thought is familiar to us. Suffering borne with faith increases our resemblance to Jesus. But the thought that by suffering we augment our union with the Body of Christ, and that we thus become the Church, perhaps surprises us. This text was doubtless inspired by a saying of St. Paul – famous, but full of mystery as well – the precise meaning of which always stands in need of being reflected upon: "I rejoice henceforth in the trials I endure for you, and I complete in my flesh what is lacking in the Passion of Christ for the sake of His Body, which is the Church." (Col 1:24) Yes, each Christian who suffers is taken up as a part of the great suffering of Christ's members. He is not alone: His suffering has an ecclesial dimension, and it constitutes a treasure from which each one of us can draw and the worth of which surpasses that of any other activity.

We certainly want, and with reason, our communities to

---

[58] Art. 118.

be holy, but also flourishing, beaming, and efficient. Now it happens sometimes that this hermitage or that is dragging itself along or seems to be almost in its death throes. But if such a situation is not the result of our unfaithfulness, and if it is accepted with humility and generosity, who can tell us that this little family "in the pangs of death" is not more agreeable to God and more useful to the world than one that sails before the wind? Making smugness an ideal makes no sense in the Christian scheme of things, for it is the realm of the glorious Cross.

Paul VI one day told the Trappists: "Do not try at all costs to make yourselves understood by people. This could lead to a deplorable dereliction of duty. Just be yourselves. God will see to it that your light shines in the eyes of men."

VIII

WHAT JOY!
CHRIST IS RISEN!

Doubtless you recall the last confession of St. Peter Damian to his disciple, John of Lodi. He seems to accuse himself in earnest, among other things, of not having had, as a cardinal and a hermit, "a gloomy enough face, and for having made too many clever remarks." Would you have expected that? He had learned from the Ancients, and from Romuald himself – that man with a festive face – and from his brethren of Fonteavellana, of whom he speaks in his Opuscule 51, that joy is a daughter of the desert. And he knew from his own experience that such joy can invade the whole being of the hermit and give him that extraordinary countenance that we sometimes encounter among our older brothers. Oh no, this is no cheap joy that you can buy commercially! It is born of the pangs of death. And yet, what a feast there is in the heart of those brothers who have it!

I can say, however, that it seems to me that this joy is one of the first principles of our vocation. The hermit, in fact, identifies completely with that man who one day is lucky enough to discover a treasure hidden in a field. "He hides it again and then goes off full of joy, sells all his goods, and buys the field." (Mt 13:44) This treasure is Jesus, before whom all else seems insignificant, and with this realization perfect joy is already beginning to dawn (Lk 2:10). You may calmly abandon all without fear of having struck a bad bargain. "I consider henceforth all as rubbish," says St. Paul, "before the sublimity of the knowledge of Christ Jesus my Lord, for whom I have left all these goods. I now regard them as rubbish in order to gain Christ and to be found in Him." (Phil 3:8ff) We feel through these words the vibrant enthusiasm of a lover. Now this is just the point: The Christian monk is essentially a lover who "prefers nothing to Christ, nothing to His love".[59] He is in a state of happiness like all the lovers of the world, filled and overflowing with elation, the *laetitia* of Psalm 121 (122). And all his deeds and gestures, his whole behavior, are going to be transfigured by it.

Taking a cursory glance at the *Rule of the Eremitical Life* published by our Brother Paul in 1520 at Camaldoli, we note with surprise the presence of this joy of love in the heart of the hermit. It is a dynamic joy stimulating him, pushing him forward, and singing through his whole being. So he does not say only that the hermit must obey his prior, in accordance with his Rule of life, but that he must "bear the yoke of obedience with joy". And here are some other beautiful examples:

"Love the profound tranquility of holy solitude."

" Savor the sweetness of retreat in cell."

"Go to Church for the work of God, not by habit or duty, but rather driven by the interior desire to praise our Creator."

"To celebrate holy Mass in the joy of the Spirit."

---

[59]   RB 72:11 and 4:21.

"To take delight in the daily practice of private recitation of the psalter."

"To rejoice in the modest measure and simplicity of food and drink."

And finally, this sums it all up: "To be happy to live at the hermitage."[60]

But I can almost hear the question most of us are asking ourselves: "How is it possible to abide lifelong in this joy at discovering and possessing the treasure?" First of all, it is true that one very quickly accustoms himself even to the most sacred aspects of our life. And who does not know that familiarity breeds contempt? And besides, the road is difficult, the door narrow, and the human heart fragile and inconstant. Love grows cold and joy seems to vanish. Nothing is more normal and even more necessary! Our eremitical life is the adventure of a love poured out into our hearts by the Holy Spirit. After the time of great strength at our departure for the desert, it is important for us to accept living daily its mystery, so that love may grow, deepen, and attain its majority and the fullness of its joy. All this takes time and patience. There ensues a spiritual combat not only against flesh and blood, but against the powers of darkness. This combat will last till death and will experience, especially in the midst of life, harsh and dreadful moments when the theological virtues will seem to sink into the abyss of nothingness. We must not be astonished and still less scandalized. Is this not the ineluctable law of death-resurrection, the law of the grain that dies in the earth to bear fruit a hundredfold? St. Peter Damian gives us the example of his cell neighbor, St.

---

[60] See also CE pp. 417-420.

Dominic Loricatus, "who bore the stigmata of Jesus in his body and whose whole life was a Good Friday. Behold him today, keeping festival and resplendent with light, celebrating in his heart the eternal glory of the Resurrection."[61]

That is why our masters strongly invite us to conversion, but also to divestment, even to "destitution", as our Brother Paul will put it. So many difficult days, and yet how precious, for they hollow out the riverbed of joy. Our Peter Damian exclaims:

> Arise then, arise O my brother, hear the summons of the apostle Paul who is there on the road you are taking. He knocks on your door, he presses you, he invites you: "Wake up, O sleeper! Arise from the dead, and Christ will enlighten you." (Eph 5:14) Since you know that Christ is risen, why would you doubt your own resurrection? Listen rather to the words proceeding from His mouth: "Whoever believes in me, even if he should die, he shall live." (Jn 11:25) So if the vivifying life wants to raise you up, why do you tolerate any longer remaining in death? Let us go, upright and valiant, into combat.[62]

This combat is nothing less than unyielding, persistent work, that little by little tears us out of the grasp of evil and the Evil One. We must resolve to do and to allow to be done everything to help heal the wounds of pride, ambition, sensuality, egoism, and anger that we carry within us, so that the new Man, who is Christ, may grow. The result will be

---

[61]   *Letter* 44:16-20.
[62]   *Sermon* 74.

freedom from all sorts of hindrances that choke the Word. These will not end up preventing us from being sons and daughters of the Resurrection who, with the Christ of Easter, "live all that they live for God", wholly gripped by glory.

What a pity that our Brother Paul should let himself go off so much into his usual "circular" contemplation while writing his famous *"Secretum meum mihi"*, after his experience of August 7, 1524, at Pascelupo in the small chapel of St. Jerome. The work is so difficult and discouraging to read for more than one of us! And yet there is, in his so deeply moving witness, an astonishingly strong freedom in the disappearance of man into God and the joy of the Risen One.

> O when, then, will it be, when Lord, that it will please You to let me taste and experience what it has pleased you to show me? When, then, will this vile creature of Yours make no more than one thing with You in an affectionate love, in a burning fire of charity? So well could Your poor creature then say: "My soul has disappeared, it is united with You in all its affections and its powers. It is drowned in You, it has let itself be submerged, it is annihilated and reduced to nothing." O how happy that soul who has been able thus to pass entirely into God, to become one with God, to drown itself completely in God, so that henceforth it is and it acts in God.[63]

It is just to this grace of annihilation, in the death-resurrection of the well-beloved Son, that the hermit aspires all along his path of perseverant waiting. And I must confess

---

[63] *Secretum Meum Mihi*, p .49.

that it is not that rare that one can discover in our hermitages, as for that matter in the charterhouse, those brothers who through their whole transfigured being greet you: "What joy! Christ is Risen!"[64] There you have, I think, the most beautiful fruit of our life.

Hiddenness has finally borne its fruit. But consider further the admirable testimony of Nazarena, our recluse sister. It will help us to continue on our marvelous adventure.

> When I found myself in my recluse cell, after the nuns had withdrawn and the door was closed, I realized with certainty that at last I was in my place, the place willed by God for me. In the course of so many years, I have never felt the temptation to leave reclusion, not even once! I have always felt joy and thanksgiving for this place God chose for me. No sacrifice has been too costly. Hidden forever with the Father, the Spirit, Jesus, and the Madonna, who has been such a great help to me for all these years, I live solely in peace. The silent solitude has lost nothing of its first enchantment, nor of the mysterious attraction of eternal newness. It is God who vivifies it. Here I am, I live in it like a fish in a lake created on purpose for it.[65]

This is exactly where hiddenness in our Desert day by day can lead us. So you too, brother – you can be transformed entirely into Joy and Light.

---

[64] Seraphim of Sarov.
[65] *Nazarena*, op. cit., p. 15.

Appendix

The Monastic Experience
of St. Romuald (+1027)

A New Interpretation of the Sources

We bring to your attention, dearest brethren, that the hermitage of Camaldoli was constructed by the holy father hermit Romuald through the inspiration of the Holy Spirit and at the request of the Most Reverend Theodald, Bishop of Arezzo, along with a church consecrated to the name of the Holy Savior in the year 1027 of His incarnation. The five cells having been constructed, the saint settled five hermit brethren in them, that is Peter and another Peter, Benedict, Giso, and Teuzo. Among these he chose Peter, also called Dagnino, a shrewd and spiritual man, and placed him as head of the other brethren. And he gave them a rule of fasting, silence, and remaining in cell.

This passage is from the so-called *Constitutions of Rudolph*,[1] a document drawn up around the year 1080 by Bl. Rudolph, fourth prior of Camaldoli. It describes the modest

---

[1] *Rodulphi Constitutiones:* RC II, 1-3.

beginnings of an important center of monastic life in central Italy.

The hermits of Alto Casentino were devoted to a kind of life dedicated exclusively to continual prayer and to pure contemplation in a climate of austere penance. In the terminology of the traditional Greek asceticism, they could be called hesychasts. To convince ourselves of this, we need only continue the reading. While some of them were living, above all, a penitential life,

> others, flying on the wings of contemplation towards the love of the heavenly fatherland, fixing their interior eye on the divine light and tasting through it, though in an incomplete manner, the ineffable sweetness, shut themselves up alone in cell. They determined to remain there until death, doing battle against the ancient enemy under the protection of God's grace.[2]

The sources

As for the writings of the founder of this eremitical community, Romuald of Ravenna, none have been preserved. One of his disciples, St. Bruno of Querfurt, composed the *Vita*, or better, the *Passione*, of the five hermits martyred in 1003 in Poland: two of them, John of Cervia and Benedict of Benevento, were the direct disciples of St. Romuald. In this *Life of the Five Brothers* [V5F], which goes back to the years 1004 to 1008, Bruno furnishes us with precious information on Romuald, who was still alive, but leaving it

---

[2]   RC III, 5.

in the background of the narration. Bruno, perhaps a relative of Otto III and a young chaplain of the imperial court, had entered the monastery of SS. Alexis and Boniface on the Aventine as a monk in 998. At that time, the monastery accommodated both Greek and Latin monks. Later on, St. Bruno became a hermit under Romuald, and then a missionary-archbishop, before he died a martyr himself in 1009 in the border zone between Poland and Lithuania. The work of Bruno, having remained unknown for centuries, was rediscovered in the 19th century. The *editio princeps* goes back to 1888.

But the principal source for the knowledge of Romuald is his *Life* [VR], a work of St. Peter Damian. It is a pearl of Christian hagiography, worthy to stand beside the lives of St. Antony, St. Benedict, and St. Nilus. It is the first work of Peter Damian, composed in 1042, or about fifteen years after the death of Romuald, which occurred in the year 1027 or the previous year.

Peter Damian, a native of Ravenna like Romuald, was scarcely twenty years old when the latter died and did not know him personally. In 1035, he entered at Fonteavellana, a small hermitage in the then diocese of Gubbio, at the foot of Mount Catria. Peter Damian does not tell us who founded Fonteavellana, but it is certain that in his time the spirit and observance of the hermitage were indebted to the personality of St. Romuald. The historians are not in agreement as to whether and to what extent Peter Damian is fully reliable in what he relates about St. Romuald. The relationship between the biographer and his subject is often rather problematic, and one easily catches the drift of his attributing to the protagonist of the story his own thoughts and ideals. In the prologue to the *Vita*, Peter Damian gives some indications on the composition of his own work. He collected the testimonies of different persons who knew the great hermit well, and perhaps he met up with monks who a few years before had read the *Life of the Five Brothers*. This would explain the coincidence of some items of information found in both writings. Peter Damian himself did not know the work of Bruno. The hermit of Fonteavellana wanted to write for spiritual edification, but without making anything up: "Our God does not need to resort to lying"[3]; and he does not pretend to be exhaustive. His narrative had had its first *Sitz im Leben* [living context] in the liturgy, that is, in the assembly of the faithful gathered around the tomb of St. Romuald each year to celebrate his transit. But the *Life of Blessed Romuald* also sets its sights on the eremitical community, to offer models of inspiration and deportment and (not last in the author's intention) to propagate the ideal of the eremitic life in the Church.

The Vocation

Romuald, son of the Duke Serge, was born around 952 into one of the most noble and powerful families of Ravenna. Young and rich, he is not yet a saint. And yet he is already devoted to God, and his biographer notes: "Each time he would fall, he would try to raise himself up and would propose to himself to achieve something great."[4] And truly, without such determination a vocation cannot

---

[3] VR, prologue.
[4] VR 1.

be realized: anybody held fast by his present situation is incapable of surrendering himself to a grand design. It is only gradually that Romuald realizes his calling to the monastic life. Involved in a private feud of his father's, in the course of which an opponent and relative meets death, Romuald, though personally innocent, takes upon himself an ecclesiastical sanction. During a penitential and reflective retreat outside the city in the monastery of St. Apollinaris in Classe, a monk of the community invites him with insistence to abandon the world. But Romuald does not give up easily: not even two apparitions of the bishop St. Apollinaris make much of an impression on him. Something very different is needed!

> Romuald was in the habit of pausing in prayer before the main altar of the Church, and there, when the monks retired, he would pray to God with much groaning. One day, while he was doing this with even greater intensity, suddenly the Holy Spirit enkindled his heart with such a great fire of divine love that he immediately burst into tears and was unable to restrain his abundant weeping. Prostrating himself at the feet of the monks, he begged, with a desire past describing, the monastic habit.[5]

The monks were quite happy to receive the offspring of so illustrious a family into the community. But the opposition of his father made the intervention of the archbishop necessary to remove all obstacles.

---

[5]   VR 2.

Cenobitic probation

Romuald stayed in this monastery for about three years. He was received as a converse, or lay brother, in the most ancient meaning of the term. While the majority of the monks in the great abbeys were "fosterlings", that is, boys educated in the monastery, one who entered as an adult was called a lay brother. Normally, the lay brothers had more practical experience of the world and were probably more motivated in their choice, but culturally they were less formed. Romuald left the world illiterate.[6]

Romuald's cenobitic experience was not too positive. In fact, he did not manage to find at St. Apollinaris a climate favorable to his deep spiritual needs. The year before he entered, the monastery had adopted the reform of Cluny, but this fact of the institutional order did not seem to elevate much the spiritual level of the monks. At least part of the confreres lived in laxity.[7] Romuald considered this situation an impediment to "undertaking the bold path of perfection to which his heart prompted him." He seriously began to ask himself what to do and was "seized by the tossing of a thousand thoughts," wrote Peter Damian.[8] In short, we are face to face with a typical vocation crisis, as old as the monastic life itself. "The demons fight the anchorites without using any weapons; instead, against the monks practicing virtue in the cenobiums and monasteries, the demons provide with weapons the most negligent among the brethren themselves,"

---

[6] VR 4.

[7] VR 3.

[8] Ibid.

thus writes Evagrius in his *Praktikos.*[9] There are at least two temptations that tend to arise. The first is discouragement. If a whole way of life leads one to nothing but a mediocre existence, without any real spiritual tension, then why commit oneself to it? But Romuald was rather tempted in the other direction: "He had the audacity to severely reprove those who were living frivolously, and often he would cite the precepts of the Rule to their confusion."[10] So he did not criticize the rule, in this case that of St. Benedict, but those who did not observe it as they should.

We saw already that Romuald had the gift of solitary and prolonged prayer. Accordingly, he used to get up before the other brethren to betake himself to church; if he found it closed he remained in prayer in the dormitory situated upstairs. His confreres, indignant against this youngster, whose behavior was for them a continuous reproof, hatched a plot to kill him by throwing him through a window. Romuald, informed of the peril, prayed to the Father in his heart of hearts to escape the impending threat. Such a state of affairs could not last: once prayer, the end of the monastic life, comes to be considered as an improper activity in a cenobium, or downright to be concealed so as not to run any risks, then the time has come to change one's very surroundings. And this Romuald does: with the consent of the abbot and the brethren – "obtained very easily" the biographer remarks – he goes off to a certain Marino, who was leading the eremitical life in the neighborhood of Venice.

---

[9] n. 5.
[10] VR 3.

Eremitic novitiate

It should be noted that this choice did not precisely correspond to what is foreseen in the first chapter of the Benedictine Rule. Romuald is not one of those who, "after a long probation in the monastery, have learnt to do battle against the devil, made expert by now with the help of many."[11] Romuald was certainly drawn to the eremitical ideal of cleaving to the Lord without distraction, but at the same time he was aware of the need of a master in order to learn still better how to live in solitude. He started what was, for all practical purposes, a second novitiate.

His new master, doubtless generous, unfortunately had not received a solid training in the eremitic life. For instance, he maintained a rather bizarre diet. The first three days of the week he kept a continuous fast, followed by a three-day diet based on cooked food and a little wine.[12] His rule of prayer was also surprising: "He used to recite the entire psalter every day with some modulation; but since he was a simple man without any instruction in the solitary life" – as Romuald himself would tell it later on with a smile – "he would very often go forth from the cell and would walk about with his disciple here and there through the extent of the hermitage, psalmodizing. Now he would intone twenty psalms under one tree, then thirty or forty under another."[13]

It seems that the program of formation at St. Apollinaris did not include the study of the psalms, and now Marino would have to fill in the gap. And this he set about doing

---

[11] *RB* 1, 4.

[12] VR 4.

[13] Ibid.

to the tune of his stick. After having taken many blows, Romuald said humbly, through constraint of necessity: "Master, please, from now on strike me on the right temple, for I am going almost completely deaf in my left ear." Then Marino, amazed at such patience, mitigated his indiscreet severity.[14]

Cuxa

The period spent in the vicinity of Venice likewise lasted about three years, and it ended with the removal of Marino and Romuald to Catalonia, to the north of the Pyrenees. Our hermits undertook this long journey together with the doge Peter Orséolo and another Venetian nobleman, John Gradenigo, under the guidance of the abbot Guarino of the monastery of St. Michael of Cuxa. This is not the place to go into the details of the political scene of Venice, whence the journey had its origin.

Marino and Romuald settled down in a hermitage in the vicinity of Cuxa, not far from Prades, at the foot of Mount Canigou. Peter and John, who at first had become monks at the monastery of the abbot Guarino, after one year joined forces with the hermits to share their austere solitude. In the meantime, Romuald became the leader of the small eremitic colony, and Marino was quite pleased to live as a disciple of Romuald, of whom shortly before he had been master.

The time spent at Cuxa, about ten years, is considered to have been fundamental for the spiritual and cultural formation of Romuald. He is no longer illiterate, but reads, among other things, the *Lives of the Fathers* and the writings

---

[14] Ibid.

of John Cassian. As the Damianian narrative continues, we find out that Romuald is a priest, but Peter Damian does not say where or when he became one. It is commonly thought that he was ordained during this period.

"Discovery" of the laura

We can easily distinguish three stages along the road traveled by Romuald up to this point. They are: cenobium – solitary eremitism – eremitism in common.

This last, in a certain sense, seems to be an arrival point, the ideal and privileged form of the monastic life as conceived by St. Romuald. He had "discovered" or renewed in Western monasticism a mode of living that was always present in the Christian East, that is, an eremitism mitigated by elements of the common life, but quite distinct from either the solitary life of a single anchorite or the cenobitic life. It seems that the technical term that designates this type of monasticism comes from sixth century Palestine: the laura. St. John Climacus, in the first chapter of the *Ladder*, recommends this form of eremitism. Also at the time of St. Nilus in southern Italy, cenobiums, hermitages, and lauras are differentiated. The latter term was little used in the Latin language, because the term "hermitage" can signify either an eremitic colony or the dwelling of a single anchorite.

Latin monasticism had always had its hermits, mentioned with reverence in the Rule of the patriarch Benedict. But the "lauratic" form of eremitism remained little recognized, if not completely unknown.

If the liturgy of the Roman Church, in the prayer for the memorial of the 19th of June, says that Romuald "renewed the eremitic life", this can only be understood in the sense of this specific form of conducting that life. The hermitage, the laura, is a structure made up of separate and non-contiguous cells, around an oratory. It is not dependent on a monastery, but rather autonomous, with its own superior and a rule to be observed by the individual members. What we have here is a semi-eremitic life oriented toward union with God in prayer, silence, and solitude. Because no essential cenobitic elements are missing in the Romualdian hermitage, it is possible to receive vocations coming directly from the world without imposing a cenobitic probation. Romuald, while still living, came to be considered as the "father of the rational hermits who lived according to rules" (*patrem rationabilium eremitarum qui cum lege vivunt*).[15] The possibility cannot be ruled out that, in some way, he may have been "infected" by Eastern monasticism precisely on this point of the preference given to a communitarian eremitism. His friend John Gradenigo said of him, "Romuald is the greatest hermit of our day, and yet he lives this beautiful and sublime life humbly, without presumption. He follows, rather, the Conferences of the desert Fathers, and so he teaches us the right way."[16]

Struggle with the demon

Numerous chapters of the *Life* refer to the struggles of Romuald with the devil, who assailed him especially at the beginning of his eremitical life. The biographer, describing the clashes with the malignant one, makes use of the

---

[15] V5F 2.

[16] Ibid.

descriptions of the tradition[17] on the one hand, and re-echoes popular accounts on the other. Like Antony, Romuald, soldier of Christ, knows no fear. "What are you driving at, you wretch! They threw you down from heaven, what are you looking for in a hermitage? Go away, dirty dog! Begone, ancient serpent!"[18] And yet, as time goes on, the aggressor in the struggle is no longer the demon, but Romuald, so much so that "the devil no longer could feel secure in attacking the saint," as Peter Damian notes.[19]

In 1088, after ten years had elapsed in French Catalonia, the hermitage next to the monastery of Cuxa was dissolved. Peter Orséolo died there and was soon venerated as a saint; Marino went to Puglia, where he met death at the hands of the Saracens, while John Gradenigo went to Monte Cassino, where he lived in the neighborhood as a hermit. Romuald returned to his monastery, but he lived in a cell that had been built in the swamp of Classe.

Here too he had to put up with the attacks of the demons, who burst into his cell:

> ...they knocked him down onto the ground, tormenting him with blows, hitting his members, exhausted by continual fasting, with big wallops. And amidst that hail of strokes Romuald, seized by the thought of divine grace, exclaimed: "Dear Jesus, beloved Jesus, why hast Thou forsaken me? Hast Thou perhaps delivered me over entirely into the hands of my enemies?"

---

[17] *Life of Antony.*
[18] VR 7.
[19] VR 61.

The weapon of the name of Jesus put the wicked spirits to flight. "Immediately, Romuald's breast was inflamed with so great a compunction of divine love that his heart melted like wax into tears and, despite the fact that his body was wounded by all those blows, he did not feel any pain."[20]

From then on, the devil changed his strategy. He would no longer confront the servant of God directly, but wherever the saint went, he would instigate the mind of his disciples against him, with a view to curbing Romuald's solicitude for the salvation of others.

No one is saved by himself

This sort of temptation presented itself in a typical fashion in the first foundation of the saint after his return to Italy, a cenobium dedicated, like Cuxa, to St. Michael, and situated on the Apennines in the diocese of Sarsina. After having established the community, Romuald lived alongside it in a solitary cell, not in the capacity of a canonical superior, but as a spiritual father, a practice he also followed successively in his other foundations.

> However, the monks of St. Michael's raged against him like wild beasts, either because, for some time, he had proven to be opposed to their habits in many respects, or because when people brought him offerings, he spent part on others instead of spending all on them. After having plotted amongst themselves, they burst all together into his cell with clubs and rods, inflicting on him many blows, taking possession of everything,

---

[20] VR 16.

and chasing him out of their land, after having
covered him with ignominy.[21]

How could we not remember the treatment suffered
by St. Benedict at the hands of the monks of Vicovaro?
The spontaneous reaction of Romuald is understandable:
for the future, he would no longer feel himself in any way
responsible for the salvation of others, satisfied only with
his own. However, writes Peter Damian, "after having had
this thought, a great fear invaded his soul: he began to dread
perishing and being condemned by the divine judgment if he
himself would really be obstinate in his resolution."[22] This is
a key text for understanding the monastic experience of St.
Romuald, as well as that of St. Peter Damian. We saw how
the experience of a mitigated eremitism was for Romuald an
essential point of his ideal. But now a second fundamental
element comes to be added: enjoying blissfully the calm
of eremitical contemplation is not sufficient, for charity
toward our neighbor demands that we strive so that others
may be saved. However, the *Vita Romualdi* leaves no doubt
about the fact that the fullness of salvation can be found in
an exclusively eremitical life. The Romualdian apostolate
consisted first of all, if not exclusively, in the "vocational
pastorate", and he did not teach sanctifying oneself by
remaining in the world. He wanted to fill with generous
souls the hermitages and monasteries he had founded, or was
yet to found.

The ardor for bearing fruit was so strong in

---

[21] VR 18.
[22] Ibid.

the heart of Romuald that he would never feel content with what he had achieved. And while still engaged in one activity, he was already poised for another. In short, it could be said that he intended to turn the whole world into a hermitage and associate all people with the monastic order.[23]

For Romuald, the hermit ought to feel responsible for the salvation of others and therefore ought to take care of others, even in the case where they prove to be hostile. Their enmity must not induce the hermit to be concerned only for himself. Peter Damian, by returning insistently many times to the rejection of Romuald by his disciples, probably wants to allude to his participation in the destiny of Jesus, above all when Romuald patiently bears the punishment for a crime he never committed.[24]

It is perhaps not superfluous to ask oneself if the polarity between hermitage and apostolate is more present in the biographer than in his subject. On this point there is, in fact, a not groundless suspicion that Peter Damian attributes to the protagonist of his narrative the preoccupations that characterize, above all, the state of his own soul. A recent study of the letters of St. Peter Damian has revealed in this hermit of Fonteavellana a clear change over the years in his conception of the monastic life: while during his first years as a hermit, he nourished the hope of a full evangelization of society through the preaching of the eremitic ideal, later this "panmonastic dream" fell through. The letters of this initial

---

[23] VR 37.
[24] VR 49 and 50.

period bear witness to the first tendency, and so, precisely, does the *Vita beati Romualdi*. After his experience as bishop, he started to harbor different ideas; in a letter written three years before his death, we read: "There was a time, it is true, in which the world needed heralds of the good news, but those times have passed. These are no longer times in which the monk could give fruitful advice and, not without good results, sow spiritual things in the minds of carnal men."[25] It is not for the hermit to actively engage in the reform of the Church and of society, taking up the duties of the hierarchy. The hermit is content not to slight the profit his hidden life affords. Remaining in his cell, he can perfectly discharge the "duty of his universality".[26]

The Romuald of the *Vita* is not reducible to a pure eremitism. He "was like one of the seraphim. He was on fire within himself with divine love beyond any comparison, and wherever he went, he inflamed others with that fire through the torch of his preaching."[27] Peter Damian adds significantly: "Often, while preaching, compunction so moved him to tears, that suddenly he would have to interrupt his discourse and flee like a madman."[28] If the gift of tears is an apex of Christian perfection, for Romuald as for Peter Damian, then eremitical preaching is neither a contradiction nor a transgression into the field of others.

---

[25] *Letter* 165.
[26] *Letter* 28.
[27] VR 35.
[28] Ibid.

Made an abbot

About the year 998, the young emperor Otto III, intending to reform the abbey of Classe, granted the monks the faculty of electing their abbot. They immediately and unanimously chose Romuald who, after having tried in vain not to take on the charge, was obliged by force to accept it. The emperor had to "drag him out of his eremitic cell".[29] Romuald "would govern his monks according to the strict discipline of the rule, and he would not permit anybody to deviate from it with impunity."[30] His abbatial experience lasted a little more than a year. The growing resistance in the community convinced Romuald to put an end to his superiorship, "which was making him lose his own quiet and purity of heart. Therefore he went to the emperor and cast the pastoral staff at his feet."[31] He did not want to be "an abbot of bodies, but of souls".[32]

Monasterialis laxitudo

The Romualdian apothegm, handed down in Letter 50 of Peter Damian, also probably reflects his experience as abbot of St. Apollinaris: "To return from the hermitage to the monastery is almost like renouncing the monastic order to return to the world." Peter Damian is of the same opinion: "Do not be pleased to descend from the rigor of the hermitage to the laxity of the monastery, and leaving the law

---

[29] V5F 2.
[30] VR 22.
[31] V5F 2.
[32] Ibid., 4.

of the spirit, to consent to the allurements of the flesh."[33] The *"districtio eremitica"* [eremitic strictness] is the expression of a complete conversion, while the *"monasterialis laxitudo"* [monastic laxity] still maintains too many ties with the world. Romuald, in particular, was very skeptical regarding the abbots of the great abbeys, which were economic and sometimes political centers. One of his successors at Apollinaris purchased the office through simony. Romuald tried to cleanse his monastery, but the abbot, besides not surrendering his post, did not scruple at making an attempt – unsuccessful – on Romuald's life.[34] "The way of life that we see prevailing today among the abbots was so abidingly odious to Romuald, that to be able to deliver an abbey from their clutches gave him the same joy as when he managed to bring one of the more powerful seculars into the monastic life."[35]

To assure a high standard of spiritual life, Romuald commanded that the abbot of his cenobitic foundations live as a hermit during the week and limit himself to seeing the community only on feasts and Sundays for the sake of teaching. This custom, which he probably learned at Pomposa, did not prove to be an efficacious remedy for the foundations at Pereo and Valdicastro.[36]

Individual eremitism

As we have observed, Romuald prefers that the hermit life be lived in small communities. But on the other hand, he

---

[33] *Letter* 18.
[34] VR 41.
[35] VR 45.
[36] Cf. VR 30 and 45.

is not completely adverse to individual eremitism, as we learn from the beautiful chapter that Peter Damian dedicates to the meeting of the master and the hermit Venerio, living in the neighborhood of Tivioli.[37] Venerio had been a cenobite whose confreres made his life impossible: "One would often beat him up, another would throw dirty water from the washing of pots on him, and still another would exasperate him by yelling all kinds of reproaches at him." Venerio then took refuge in solitude, leading a very rigorous and austere life. When Romuald met him, he asked him what authority he was under. Venerio replied that he was without a superior and did whatever he thought best. Romuald replied: "If you are bearing the cross of Christ, you must go still further and not omit the obedience of Christ. So go, get your abbot's consent. Then return and live humbly submissive to him." Implicitly – given that inconsistency can be ruled out – these words inform us that Romuald himself, "within whose heart the Holy Spirit presided",[38] would travel and work in obedience to an authority not specified in the Damianian account.

Reclusion

Romualdian semi-eremitism would be incomplete without the possibility of reclusion in the bosom of the eremitic community. Many times, Peter Damian presents Romuald himself as a recluse for periods more or less protracted, for instance, two years in Istria and seven at Sitria. Reclusion, confronted in view of a superior freedom,

---

[37] VR 24.
[38] V5F 4.

is a death to the world[39] and entails the observance of strict silence. "Ever silent of tongue and preaching by his life, he was able to engage himself, as almost never before, for both the benefit of men wanting to live a life of conversion and those hastening to repentance."[40] "The recluse is indeed separated from all, and at the same time, united to all," according to the well-known expression of Evagrius.[41] From the times of Romuald until our days, reclusion is an essential element of Romualdian eremitism. It realizes, in a precise and extreme form, what St. Benedict, in the first chapter of his Rule, foresees for the eremitic vocation: an exceptional vocation, in any case, a "vocation within a vocation", so to speak, similar in this respect to martyrdom.

Martyrdom

Bruno of Querfurt sees the "supereminence" of the semi-eremitic life not in reclusion, of which he does not write, but in the evangelization of the pagans in view of a cruel martyrdom, as it was realized in the Five Brothers and later on in Bruno himself. In his writing, Bruno attributes to the Emperor Otto a missionary project that is at the same time an ascetical project.

> The plan was to construct a monastery among the Christians, but near to pagan territory, in a place set apart, surrounded by woods. This would offer a triple advantage: community life, which beginners desire; golden solitude for the

---

[39] VR 64.
[40] VR 52.
[41] *De oratione,* 124.

mature, thirsting for the living God; and the announcement of the Gospel among the pagans, for those who yearn to be set free and to be with Christ.[42]

It cannot be affirmed that we have here a program worked out by Romuald, nor would it be accurate to identify the *"evangelium paganorum"* [evangelization of the pagans] with a modern pastoral apostolate.

Beyond any doubt, martyrdom constitutes the supreme way of corresponding to the love of Christ unto the end. But it is an exceptional grace, which cannot be the supreme goal of an ascetical program.

When two of Romuald's dearest and most worthy disciples declared their intention to depart for Poland, he was little inclined to let them leave. "He did not know what might be the will of God on a matter so charged with risk, and therefore he wanted to submit it to the decision of the brethren rather than to his own."[43] However, some years later, "when he found out that Boniface (i.e., Bruno of Querfurt) had received martyrdom, Romuald felt on fire with a great desire to pour out his blood for Christ and very quickly decided to go to Hungary."[44] So he left with the permission of the Apostolic See, together with twenty-four brothers, of which two were consecrated archbishops, and "in all was the zeal to die for Christ."[45] When they reached Hungarian territory, Romuald unexpectedly fell ill. He had scarcely decided to turn back, when he was instantly healed.

---

[42] V5F 4.
[43] VR 28.
[44] VR 39.
[45] Ibid.

But once he resumed the journey in the direction of Hungary, the illness quickly struck him once more, and this happened several times. Then Romuald understood that God did not want for him the mission and the cruel martyrdom, and he returned with part of the group. Of the others, none attained martyrdom, as St. Romuald had foreseen. Peter Damian comments: "By virtue of his intention, he achieved martyrdom at once."[46] To live like the true hermits was traditionally considered an "*imitatio martyrum*", a concept well known to Peter Damian: "A golden age was that of Romuald! Although the tortures of persecutors were absent, nevertheless voluntary martyrdom was not lacking!"[47]

Hermit on the road

Romuald was glad to be insulted, derided, and denigrated, so long as he had nothing on his conscience to reproach him.[48] And in fact, not all admired him. One of the points that might have seemed to prove his critics right must have been his continual change of residence. To call this an itinerant eremitism is excessive, but his travels in Italy and abroad are truly exceptional. No wonder his "biographers" felt themselves obliged to defend Romuald from accusations of instability.

> Hearing talk of all these relocations of the saint, one should take care not to attribute them to the vice of flightiness, when instead they proceeded from the seriousness of his religious activity.

[46] Ibid.
[47] VR 64.
[48] V5F 4.

Indisputably, his moving about was motivated by the fact that, wherever Romuald stayed, an almost countless mob of people would rush to him. So common sense demanded that, once it was ascertained that a place was full and a superior named, he would hurry on to fill another place.[49]

In the evening of his existence, St. Romuald could have made St. Nilus' words his own: "I have been a pilgrim all the days of my life."

The gift of tears

Romuald met up with countless people during the course of his life, but his true traveling companion was Jesus. What bestows a profound unity upon his busy and eventful life is a tender love for the Savior. Perhaps the most characteristic expression of this love is the tears that the saint shed abundantly not only in cell or in church, but on various occasions, even on horseback![50] It is especially the beautiful Chapter 31 of the *Vita* that shows us the mystical Romuald. After the dissolution of the hermitage of Pereo in 1001, Romuald withdrew to Istria, where he had founded a monastery in the territory of Parenzo (Porec), and he lived there for two years as a recluse. "While he was staying at Parenzo, he was sometimes distressed by the desire to burst into tears. Yet try as he might, he was incapable of attaining the compunction of a contrite heart." It is necessary to keep in mind that, at that time, sacramental confession was little used, and the certainty that God had forgiven one's sins came

---

[49] VR 49.
[50] VR 35.

precisely from the shedding of tears. They are in the strict sense a grace, a sign of forgiveness.

> Unexpectedly, there arose so ample an outpouring of tears, and his mind was so illuminated in the understanding of the divine Scriptures, that from that day on for the rest of his life, he could shed abundant tears easily whenever he wished, and the spiritual sense of Scripture was no longer hidden from him.

The deepest sense of the Scriptures is Jesus Christ, that is to say, the foolish love of God for man in need of His mercy. To become aware of this, and to shed abundant tears, is all one.

> Often he would remain so rapt in the contemplation of God that he would be dissolved almost entirely into tears. And as he burned with an unspeakable ardor of divine love, it would emerge in exclamations like these: "Dear Jesus, beloved! My sweet honey, inexpressible desire, sweetness of the saints, delightfulness of the angels!" Words which, under the dictation of the Holy Spirit, would turn into jubilation for him. . . .

How could this not call to mind his contemporary, St. Simeon the New Theologian, in the imperial city on the Bosphorus!

Henceforth, the gift of tears became habitual for him, so much so that he believed in his simplicity that God granted this same grace to all. Therefore, he would repeat often to his disciples: "Be careful not to shed too many tears, for they ruin one's sight and damage the brain."

Psalmody

Romuald loved to recite the psalms. He passed on this love to his disciples:

> If you have arrived recently, and despite your first fervor do not manage to pray as you would wish, seek here and there to chant the psalms in your heart and to understand them with your mind. When some distractions arise, do not stop reading; return hastily to the text, and apply your intelligence again.[51]

He plainly gave preference to the quality of the psalmody: "It is better, if possible, to say a single psalm from the heart and with compunction, than to run through a hundred of them with a wandering mind."[52] Cassian, before him, had been of the same opinion: "It is more suitable to chant only ten verses of a psalm with concentration of mind than to run distractedly through the whole psalter."[53] Romuald must have been a diligent expert in the psalms, so much so that he was ordered by the Lord Himself to compose a commentary on them. Unfortunately, his commentary has not come down to us. Peter Damian could still consult it, and he found it excellent: "Although Romuald made grammatical mistakes, he always gathered the meaning."[54]

---

[51] V5F 19.
[52] VR 9.
[53] *Institutes* 2, 11.
[54] VR 50.

Hesychastic prayer

"Although the saint made use of much austerity on himself, yet he would always show a cheerful countenance, a serene appearance."[55] Asceticism is not an absolute value, but it serves for the purification of the heart and of prayer. "If one is stretching forward toward prayer," he used to say, "it is particularly advantageous to eat every day and to always remain a bit hungry."[56]

Romuald did not write a rule in the strict sense of the word. He insisted on the observance of the Benedictine Rule for monasteries, while for hermitages the rules were handed down orally.[57] But his disciple John, later a martyr in Poland, received from him a "little rule" of sharp contemplative, hesychastic flavor. It contains twice the invitation to remain seated. This is the position of Mary of Bethany at the feet of Jesus, the typical position of the hesychasts, certainly not adopted to make them comfortable, but rather humble and attentive. "Sit in your cell as in paradise. Forget the world and cast it behind your back. Be attentive to your thoughts like a good fisherman to the fish."[58] Somebody wanted to see in this comparison a recollection of Romuald as fisherman in the Po delta; that is possible, but we have here an image often used by the Eastern Fathers, for instance by John Climacus: "The vigilant monk is a fisher of thoughts who, in the tranquility of the night, easily knows how to spot them and

---

[55] VR 53.
[56] VR 9.
[57] Cf. RC II,3.
[58] V5F 19.

is able to catch them."[59] It is, in fact, the ancient experience of monks that prayer (*proseuchē*) is to a great extent the fruit of attention (*prosochē*) to the movements of the mind.

The "little rule" continues: "First of all, put yourself in the presence of God with fear and trembling, like one standing before the emperor." To tell the truth, Romuald himself did not show "fear and trembling" before the emperors Otto III, Henry II, and other potentates, but rather the attitude of outspokenness, of "*parrhesia*".[60] This is not a contradiction: such an attitude is, in fact, only possible for those who profoundly humble themselves before God, recognizing their own nothingness. "In order to obey God in everything, [Romuald] had no fear of displeasing men."[61] The "little rule" concludes: "Annihilate yourself and sit like a baby, content with the grace of God; if God does not give it to you like a mother, you will taste nothing and have nothing to eat." It is moving to see how this rough ascetic sends us back to spiritual infancy and to the "maternity" of God, stressing in this way the absolute primacy of Grace.

Camaldoli again

The hermitages and monasteries springing from the initiative of the Ravennese hermit had no canonical bond among them, nor did they constitute an institution. So it would not be exact to define Romuald as "Founder of the Camaldolese Order". His foundations, including those of

---

[59] *Ladder* 20.
[60] Cf. T. Merton, *The New Man* (1961), fourth essay.
[61] VR 22.

a cenobitic character, were rather modest in size and, for the most part, short-lived. An exception was the hermitage of Camaldoli, the most successful and certainly the most enduring work of the saint.

It is quite surprising that Peter Damian does not make mention of Camaldoli in the *Vita Romualdi*. At the time he was writing, he probably did not yet know the place. Situated in the Tuscan-Romagnan Apennines in the midst of a forest of fir trees, and more than a thousand meters in altitude, the locality must have seemed undisturbed and difficult of access.

> The pious Romuald, father of hermits, chose this place and deemed it most suitable and convenient for the little cells of the brother hermits who serve God alone in the contemplative life. Having built in the same place the Church of the Holy Savior, there he likewise marked off five small cells, each with its own oratory, separated from one another. To the individual cells he assigned individual brother hermits who, abandoning the cares and preoccupations of the secular life, applied themselves only to divine contemplation.[62]

In order to render separation from the peopled world still more clear-cut, a dependent house, Fonte Bono, was built at the same time at a distance of three kilometers further downhill. It served as guesthouse and hospice, and as a place for the material administration. A monk and three lay brothers resided there. Some historians see in these lay religious the beginning of the institution of lay brothers in Latin monasticism.

---

[62] Document of Bishop Theodald of Arezzo of August 1, 1027.

The document of Theodald, quoted above, intended authoritatively to prevent that Camaldoli in time would become a cenobium: "We order that the brethren who, in the course of time, serve God in that place, never lead a life different from that eremitic, solitary, and contemplative life. And it shall not be permitted them that this holy place degenerate into a monastery of cenobites." For in fact, it did not infrequently happen that an eremitic colony lost over time its original character and was turned into a monastery. If Camaldoli remained for divers centuries a place of authentic eremitic life, this is due in great part to Bishop Theodald and his successors, who judged the existence of the hermits, dedicated to silence, fasting, and perseverance in the cell, of irreplaceable value for their local Church. Perhaps the history of the first fifty years of Camaldoli brings out better the deep intentions of St. Romuald than does Peter Damian who, with his strong personality, certainly sheds light upon some aspects of the figure of Romuald, but partly leaves other aspects in the shade.

The mystery of Romuald

One cannot deny that there exists a tension between the Romuald *"sterilitatis impatiens"* [impatient with barrenness] and the Romuald who sits in the cell as in paradise – or likewise between the Romuald who at Valdicastro preaches against simoniacal priests and bishops, and the founder of Camaldoli. "In the world the hermitage attracts Romuald; in the hermitage the world is constantly present," writes John Tabacco. Certainly, in other times the standards for judging certain kinds of behavior were different from today's, and today we hold incompatible that which then was not so considered.

At any rate, it was almost to be expected that after the death of such a father, his sons could not but litigate by reason of the inheritance. So even though the historical Romuald is only one, each of the two branches of the Camaldolese present in the Church today sees their father in a different light, starting with the habit: There is a Romuald wearing an ample cowl worthy of a baroque abbot, and there is a Romuald whose poor mantle scarcely reaches below his knees. The first can be defined as a "pluralist", intent on realizing the completeness of the monastic charism, which includes, besides the cloistered life, a multiplicity of services for the benefit of the local and universal Church as well. And then there is the other Romuald, who in an essential and profound way is a hermit, but who takes up other works – aware of the needs of the historical moment, and given the absence, in that epoch, of religious especially dedicated to the pastoral life.

Today, by the grace of God, such religious exist and permit the hermit to dedicate himself to the "one thing necessary" (Lk 10:42), that is, to cultivate his proper vocation of penance, prayer, and contemplation. He is aware of the fact that his vocation also constitutes a service, and the Church of God would gravely feel the effects of the lack of it. "The hermits," writes the Holy Father John Paul II in *Vita Consecrata* (n.42), "in the depth of solitude, not only do not subtract from the ecclesial community, but they serve it with their specific contemplative charism."

Sacro Eremo Tuscolano   5 September 2004

CPSIA information can be obtained
at www.ICGtesting.com
Printed in the USA
BVHW031753120919
558277BV00003B/287/P